Proverbs for the 21st Century

A Study of the Book of Proverbs for Today's Chaotic Lives

Debb Boom Wateren

Table of Contents

Introduction

In an age marked by rapid change and unceasing challenges, the timeless wisdom of the Book of Proverbs continues to illuminate our path, offering guidance and insight for the 21st century. Welcome to "Proverbs for the 21st Century: A Guide to Wisdom for Young Adults and Adults."

Proverbs, often referred to as the "Book of Wisdom," is a treasure trove of ageless principles for living a fulfilling and purposeful life. Its teachings transcend the boundaries of culture, time, and age, making it as relevant today as it was thousands of years ago. Within its verses, we find pearls of wisdom that can guide us through the complexities of our modern world.

This book is an invitation to embark on a journey of discovery and transformation. It's a journey that will take you through the ancient words of Proverbs, while simultaneously connecting them to the pressing issues and choices you face in your daily life. As we delve into the wisdom of this timeless book, we will explore its profound insights on relationships, work, communication, character, and much more. We will examine how these insights can empower you to navigate the challenges of our time with grace, integrity, and a heart full of compassion.

In the following pages, you'll find a comprehensive guide designed for young adults and adults alike. Each chapter explores a key aspect of the Book of Proverbs and unpacks its significance for our contemporary world. Through meaningful discussions, practical exercises, and thought-provoking questions, you will have the opportunity to engage with the material on a deep and personal level. Whether you're exploring Proverbs for the first time or revisiting its wisdom with fresh eyes, this book is crafted to meet you where you are on your spiritual and life journey.

The book is also designed to use the New Living Translation of the Bible. A translation that is written in contemporary English and designed for the 21st Century. Please be advised that this translation is a thought-for-thought ideology and is less accurate than a literal translation like the New American Standard or the English Standard Version. Therefore, feel free to incorporate any translation of the Bible that you prefer.

But our journey doesn't end with the final chapter. In the "Suggestions for Future Study" section, you'll discover resources and recommendations for further exploration and continued growth. We hope that this book will serve as a stepping stone, inspiring you to dive deeper into the well of wisdom and faith.

Wisdom is a lifelong pursuit, and it has the power to transform your life, your relationships, and your place in the world. It is our sincere wish that "Proverbs for the 21st Century" becomes a trusted companion as you seek to embody the wisdom and values found in this ancient book in your modern life.

Let's embark on this journey together, and may the wisdom of Proverbs illuminate your path and guide your steps in the 21st century.

This study uses the New Living Translation. Copyright 2015 by Tyndale House Foundation

Get Ready for Group Discussions

- Listen to others with love.

- Listen to others from your heart. Try to understand the heart of what others are sharing.

- Listen to others with a non-judgmental attitude. You may disagree, but you can affirm that person's right to a different point of view.

- Listen to others with respect for their freedom. The group does not exist to give advice, but to encourage growth. We do not have to be of one voice or one mind.

- Listen to others with shared trust. A basic level of trust encourages sharing beyond the superficial. All sharing must be kept confidential.

- Speak from your own experience. Use the pronoun "I" when you share your point of view.

Overview of the Book of Proverbs

Structure and Authorship:

Themes

The Nature of Wisdom:

Moral and Ethical living:

The Power of Words:

Work, Diligence, and Wealth:

Relationships:

Fear of the Lord:

3

Chapter 1: Understanding the Book of Proverbs

Overview of the Book of Proverbs

The Book of Proverbs is a profound and practical collection of wisdom literature found in the Hebrew Bible (the Old Testament) and forms a vital part of the religious and moral heritage of both Judaism and Christianity. At its core, Proverbs is a guide to living a wise, righteous, and meaningful life, offering timeless insights into human behavior, morality, and the pursuit of wisdom.

Structure and Authorship: Traditionally, King Solomon, known for his legendary wisdom, is attributed as the primary author of many of the Proverbs. However, the book is a compilation of wise sayings, maxims, and poems attributed to various authors. It is structured in a way that reflects a father's advice to his son, creating a mentor-student relationship throughout the text. The book is divided into 31 chapters, making it suitable for daily reading over a month.

Themes
The Nature of Wisdom: Proverbs emphasizes that wisdom is the principal thing. It urges readers to seek wisdom above all else, recognizing that it brings understanding, discretion, and discernment in life's decisions.

Moral and Ethical Living: A significant portion of Proverbs is dedicated to exploring the concepts of righteousness, justice, and ethical living. It encourages readers to live a life of integrity, honesty, and kindness.

The Power of Words: The book addresses the profound impact of our words and the importance of using speech wisely. Proverbs extols the value of truthful and gracious communication while cautioning against destructive speech.

Work, Diligence, and Wealth: Proverbs guide diligence in one's work and the responsible management of resources. It acknowledges the pursuit of prosperity while emphasizing the importance of doing so with fairness and generosity.

Relationships: Proverbs offers insights into various types of relationships, including family, friendships, and marriage. It stresses the significance of loyalty, trust, and empathy in building strong connections.

Fear of the Lord: A central theme in Proverbs is the fear of the Lord, which is often regarded as a reverence for God and an acknowledgment of divine guidance. This theme underscores the spiritual foundation of wisdom.

Application to the 21st Century: Despite being written in ancient times; the Book of Proverbs remains remarkably relevant in the 21st century. Its teachings provide timeless guidance for navigating the complexities of modern life, from decision-making and interpersonal relationships to financial stewardship and moral conduct. The wisdom found in Proverbs continues to serve as a source of inspiration and moral compass for those seeking a life of purpose, integrity, and virtue.

In "Proverbs for the 21st Century: A Guide to Wisdom for Young Adults and Adults," we will explore these timeless principles and apply them to the challenges and opportunities of our contemporary world. Through reflection, discussion, and practical exercises, this book aims to help readers unlock the wisdom contained within the Book of Proverbs and integrate it into their lives, fostering personal growth, enriching relationships, and nurturing a deeper connection with the divine.

Historical and Cultural Context of the Book of Proverbs

Understanding the historical and cultural context of the Book of Proverbs is essential for interpreting and appreciating the wisdom it imparts. Proverbs is a product of its time and culture, and this context greatly influences the themes and messages within the book.

Ancient Israel: The Book of Proverbs is firmly rooted in the context of ancient Israel. It was written during a time when the Israelites were grappling with the challenges of nation-building, political transitions, and the quest for a distinct identity as the chosen people of God. The book reflects the values, beliefs, and societal norms of this ancient civilization.

Wisdom Literature: Proverbs belong to a broader genre of biblical literature known as "wisdom literature." Other wisdom books in the Bible include Job, Ecclesiastes, and parts of Psalms and Song of Solomon. Wisdom literature was a common genre in the ancient Near East, and it often contained practical advice, philosophical reflections, and insights into the nature of the world and human existence.

Influence of Surrounding Cultures: The culture and literature of ancient Israel were influenced by neighboring civilizations, such as Egypt and Mesopotamia. This influence is evident in the similarities between some Proverbs and the wisdom literature of these neighboring cultures. However, Proverbs also contains distinct theological and ethical elements that set it apart.

Authorship and Compilation: Proverbs is traditionally attributed to King Solomon, renowned for his wisdom. While Solomon is credited with many of the proverbs, the book also includes contributions from other sages and writers. This diverse authorship is reflected in the varied themes and styles throughout the book.

Societal Structure: The society depicted in Proverbs is hierarchical, with clear distinctions between rulers, nobles, common people, and servants. This social structure is reflected in the book's advice on respecting authority, the responsibilities of leaders, and the virtues of humility.

Oral Tradition: In ancient Israel, knowledge and wisdom were often passed down through oral tradition. Proverbs were likely part of this tradition, with these sayings being taught, memorized, and recited by individuals within families and communities.

The Fear of the Lord: A central theme in Proverbs is the "fear of the Lord," which encompasses reverence for God and the acknowledgment of divine guidance. This concept was integral to the religious and moral fabric of ancient Israel, and it underpins many of the book's teachings.

Symbolism and Imagery: Proverbs often employ vivid and symbolic language to convey their messages. The use of imagery drawn from daily life, nature, and agriculture was a common feature of Hebrew poetry and wisdom literature.

Understanding the historical and cultural context of the Book of Proverbs allows readers to grasp the significance of the book's teachings within the framework of its time. It provides valuable insights into the challenges and aspirations of ancient Israel and offers a foundation for applying the book's wisdom to the contemporary world, as we explore in "Proverbs for the 21st Century: A Guide to Wisdom for Young Adults and Adults."

Themes and Purposes of the Book of Proverbs

The Book of Proverbs is a rich source of wisdom and guidance, filled with numerous themes and purposes that continue to resonate with readers today. These themes and purposes offer profound insights into human behavior, morality, and the pursuit of wisdom.

The Pursuit of Wisdom: The primary theme of Proverbs is the pursuit of wisdom. It emphasizes that wisdom is the most valuable possession one can attain. The book encourages readers to seek wisdom with zeal, understanding that it brings clarity, discretion, and insight into life's complex decisions. The pursuit of wisdom is not only an intellectual endeavor but also a moral and spiritual one.

Moral and Ethical Living: A significant portion of Proverbs is dedicated to the theme of moral and ethical living. It offers practical advice on how to live a life characterized by righteousness, integrity, and ethical conduct. Proverbs is filled with admonitions to be just, honest, and virtuous in all aspects of life.

The Power of Words: Proverbs highlights the profound impact of words and speech. It encourages readers to use their words wisely, emphasizing the importance of truth, kindness, and gracious communication. It also warns against the destructive power of deceitful or hurtful speech.

Work, Diligence, and Wealth: Proverbs addresses the importance of diligence and hard work in various aspects of life, including one's occupation and the management of wealth. It acknowledges the pursuit of prosperity while urging readers to do so with fairness, generosity, and a focus on ethical business practices.

Relationships: Proverbs provide insights into various types of relationships, including family, friendships, and marriage. It offers guidance on building and maintaining healthy, strong, and loving relationships. The book highlights the importance of qualities like loyalty, trust, empathy, and forgiveness in human connections.

The Fear of the Lord: A central theme in Proverbs is the "fear of the Lord," which refers to reverence for God and an acknowledgment of divine guidance in all aspects of life. This theme underscores the spiritual foundation of wisdom and moral living.

Instruction and Guidance: Proverbs serve as a manual for instruction and guidance in daily life. It offers practical, day-to-day advice on how to navigate the challenges and opportunities that arise in one's personal, social, and professional life.

Personal Growth and Character Development: The book encourages personal growth and character development, highlighting the importance of qualities like humility, self-control, and integrity. It underscores the idea that wisdom is not merely theoretical knowledge but something that should be embodied in one's character.

Divine Order and Justice: Proverbs often reflect the belief in a divine order that governs human affairs and the universe. It emphasizes that good deeds are rewarded and wrongdoing ultimately leads to suffering or consequences. This theme provides a moral and spiritual context for the book's teachings.

The overarching purpose of the Book of Proverbs is to impart practical, moral, and spiritual wisdom that can guide individuals in living meaningful and righteous lives. Its themes and purposes aim to help readers make informed decisions, build strong relationships, succeed in their endeavors, and cultivate a deep reverence for God. The book's enduring relevance is a testament to the timeless nature of its wisdom, which continues to enrich and inspire people's lives in the 21st century and beyond.

Interpreting Proverbs for the 21st Century

The Book of Proverbs, with its ancient wisdom, can appear at first glance to be a collection of timeless maxims with little connection to the complexities of the 21st century. However, a thoughtful and contemporary interpretation of Proverbs reveals its enduring relevance and its potential to guide individuals in the modern world. Here are some key principles for interpreting Proverbs for the 21st century:

Recognize the Universal Truths: While the cultural and historical context of Proverbs is ancient, the underlying truths it conveys are universal. Principles of ethical living, the power of words, the pursuit of wisdom, and the importance of strong relationships are as relevant today as they were thousands of years ago. Recognize these timeless truths and consider how they apply to modern life.

Contextualize the Advice: Proverbs often provide advice for specific situations, but the situations themselves may not be directly applicable to contemporary life. Instead of taking proverbs at face value, seek to understand the underlying principles. For example, a proverb about agricultural practices can be understood as a metaphor for the principles of diligence and careful planning in one's work or personal life.

Embrace Flexibility and Nuance: Interpreting Proverbs requires a flexible mindset. While some proverbs offer clear-cut guidance, others are more open to interpretation. Embrace nuance and recognize that there may not be one-size-fits-all answers to complex modern dilemmas. Wisdom often involves making judgments that consider various factors and perspectives.

Bridge the Gap Between Ancient and Modern Cultures: To make Proverbs relevant to the 21st century, it's essential to bridge the cultural gap between the ancient world and today. Consider how the wisdom in Proverbs aligns with contemporary values, ethical standards, and societal norms. Recognize where it may conflict, challenge, or complement modern thought.

Apply Proverbs Reflectively: Proverbs are not meant to be rigid rules but rather sources of reflection. Encourage readers to think critically about how the wisdom of Proverbs can be applied to their unique situations and challenges. Encourage them to adapt the principles to their own lives while respecting the essence of the wisdom.

Emphasize Personal Growth: Interpreting Proverbs for the 21st century should prioritize personal growth and character development. Encourage readers to use the wisdom found in Proverbs as a framework for self-improvement and ethical living. Proverbs should inspire individuals to become wiser, more compassionate, and better decision-makers.

Encourage Dialogue and Discussion: Proverbs can be a starting point for meaningful discussions on moral and ethical topics. Interpretation for the 21st century should encourage dialogue and reflection, both in personal study and in group settings. Engaging with others to explore the wisdom of Proverbs can lead to deeper understanding and practical application.

Adapt for Contemporary Challenges: Modern challenges, such as technology, globalization, and changing societal dynamics, present new ethical dilemmas and opportunities. Interpret Proverbs to address these challenges. Seek to apply the wisdom to issues like digital ethics, environmental stewardship, and social justice.

In "Proverbs for the 21st Century: A Guide to Wisdom for Young Adults and Adults," the interpretation of Proverbs is not about reimagining or distorting the ancient wisdom but about discovering how these ageless principles can illuminate the path of individuals living in a rapidly evolving world. By bridging the ancient and the modern, readers can find in Proverbs a wellspring of guidance that enriches their lives and empowers them to navigate the complex landscape of the 21st century with wisdom and grace.

Questions for Individual Use or Group Discussion

1 - How can the principles of Proverbs assist us in making ethically sound decisions in a world filled with complex moral dilemmas?

2 - What insights from Proverbs can we apply to foster stronger and more meaningful relationships in an age where digital communication often replaces face-to-face interaction?

3 - In an era of instant communication and social media, how can we apply Proverbs' teachings on the power of words to promote healthier online and offline dialogue?

4 - How can the character development principles from Proverbs help us adapt and grow in a world that demands continuous personal and professional development?

5 - How can Proverbs' wisdom guide us in facing contemporary challenges, including those related to mental health, work-life balance, and social justice?

6 - In what ways can the wisdom of Proverbs be adapted to address current issues like environmental stewardship, digital ethics, and global interconnectedness?

7 - How can we reconcile the ageless wisdom of Proverbs with the dynamic changes and innovations of the 21st century to lead a balanced and purposeful life?

8 - How does the Book of Proverbs continue to resonate with contemporary cultural and spiritual values, and what makes it a valuable guide for individuals of diverse backgrounds and beliefs?

9 - How can the wisdom contained in Proverbs stimulate meaningful dialogue and reflection among individuals and communities in the modern world, fostering greater understanding and empathy?

Note to the leader for group discussion. These critical thinking questions encourage readers to explore the enduring significance of Proverbs in the 21st century. By engaging with these questions, readers can establish the importance of applying the book's wisdom to navigate the complexities, challenges, and opportunities of the contemporary world, fostering personal growth, ethical living, and meaningful relationships.

Chapter 2: Applying Proverbs in the Modern World

In Chapter 2 of "Proverbs for the 21st Century: A Guide to Wisdom for Young Adults and Adults," we embark on a journey to bridge the timeless wisdom of the Book of Proverbs with the complexities of our modern world. This chapter is dedicated to the practical application of Proverbs' profound insights, offering a roadmap for how its ancient wisdom can guide us in navigating the challenges, dilemmas, and opportunities of the 21st century.

The Book of Proverbs is replete with timeless truths and ageless principles, but it often requires thoughtful interpretation and adaptation to resonate with contemporary life. In this chapter, we will delve into the practical aspects of Proverbs, exploring how its teachings can enrich our daily existence, influence our decision-making, and contribute to our personal growth.

As we journey through these pages, we will consider Proverbs as more than just an ancient collection of maxims; it is a practical guide that encourages us to grapple with the intricacies of modern living. We will discuss how its wisdom applies to the ethical dilemmas we encounter, the personal and professional decisions we must make, and the challenges and joys of building meaningful relationships.

This chapter aims to equip you with the tools to engage with Proverbs in a way that transcends mere intellectual understanding. It's about making its wisdom an integral part of your daily life, enabling you to become a wiser, more ethical, and more compassionate individual in the 21st century.

So, as we journey through the practical applications of Proverbs, let's open our minds to the profound insights that this age-old book offers. Let's discover how its teachings can guide us on a path of wisdom, ethical living, and meaningful connections in the modern world.

Proverbs 1 and Wisdom in Everyday Life

The pursuit of wisdom is not an abstract, esoteric endeavor confined to lofty philosophies and ancient texts; it is a practical and transformative journey that finds its relevance in everyday life. Proverbs 1, the opening chapter of the Book of Proverbs, provides us with a poignant example of how wisdom can be integrated into our daily existence, offering valuable lessons that transcend time and culture.

Let the wise listen to these proverbs and become even wiser. Let those with understanding receive guidance. - 1:5

Proverbs 1:5 begins with the proclamation, "Let the wise listen and become even wiser." In the hustle and bustle of our modern world, where information inundates us from every direction, the importance of active listening and continual learning is more pertinent than ever. Wisdom encourages us to embrace the discipline of attentive listening and to remain open to new knowledge and experiences, no matter our age or stage in life.

Proverbs 1:5 also encourages us to seek understanding, which is far more than mere knowledge. Understanding requires insight, discernment, and the ability to apply wisdom to real-life situations. In an era where information is readily available, seeking true understanding is paramount in making informed and ethical decisions.

Fear of the Lord is the foundation of true knowledge, but fools despise wisdom and discipline. - 1:7

The fear of the Lord is often understood as a profound reverence for the divine and a recognition of God's guidance in our lives. This spiritual component of wisdom remains a timeless foundation for ethical living, anchoring us in a world that often seems adrift.

My child, listen when your father corrects you. Don't neglect your mother's instruction. - 1:8

This chapter also highlights the significance of parental guidance and the passing down of wisdom from one generation to the next. Proverbs 1:8 advises, "Listen, my son, to your father's instruction and do not forsake your mother's teaching." In today's world, where familial bonds and traditional values may sometimes be strained, the timeless wisdom of respecting and learning from our elders remains invaluable.

My child, if sinners entice you, turn your back on them! They may say, "Come and join us. Let's hide and kill someone! Just for fun, let's ambush the innocent! Let's swallow them alive, like the grave let's swallow them whole, like those who go down to the pit of death. Think of the great things we'll get! We'll fill our houses with all the stuff we take. Come, throw in your lot with us; we'll all share the loot." My child, don't go along with them! Stay far away from their paths. They rush to commit evil deeds. They hurry to commit murder. If a bird sees a trap being set, it knows to stay away. But these people set an ambush for themselves; they are trying to get themselves killed. Such is the fate of all who are greedy for money; it robs them of life. - 1:10-19

Proverbs 1:10-19 offers a stark warning about the dangers of succumbing to peer pressure and making unwise associations. The text cautions against joining those who would lead us astray. In our 21st-century context, where the allure of social conformity and peer influence have taken on new forms, Proverbs 1 reminds us of the enduring importance of surrounding ourselves with wise, morally grounded individuals.

Wisdom shouts in the streets. She cries out in the public square. She calls to the crowds along the main street, to those gathered in front of the city gate: "How long, you simpletons, will you insist on being simpleminded? How long will you mockers relish your mocking? How long will you fools hate knowledge? Come and listen to my counsel. I'll share my heart with you and make you wise. "I called you so often, but you wouldn't come. I reached out to you, but you paid no attention. You ignored my advice and rejected the correction I offered. So, I will laugh when you are in trouble! I will mock you when disaster overtakes you—when calamity overtakes you like a storm, when disaster engulfs you like a cyclone, and anguish and distress overwhelm you. "When they cry for help, I will not answer. Though they anxiously search for me, they will not find me. For they hated knowledge and chose not to fear the Lord. They rejected my advice and paid no attention when I corrected them. Therefore, they must eat the bitter fruit of living their own way, choking on their own schemes. For simpletons turn away from me—to death. Fools are destroyed by their own complacency. - 1:20-32

The consequences of foolish decisions are explored in Proverbs 1:20-32, where wisdom's call is spurned, and folly is embraced. These verses emphasize the importance of recognizing that choices have outcomes. In our world filled with choices, Proverbs 1 serves as a sobering reminder to consider the potential consequences of our actions and to choose wisely.

In sum, Proverbs 1 offers a compelling example of how wisdom is not an abstract concept but a practical guide for daily life. Its teachings about listening, learning, making choices, seeking understanding, and honoring the divine remind us that wisdom is a vital companion on our journey through the complexities of the 21st century. When we apply these principles, we tap into the timeless wisdom of Proverbs, enriching our lives and enhancing our ability to navigate the challenges and opportunities of today's world with grace and insight.

Proverbs 2 and Decision-Making

Proverbs 2, a continuation of the wisdom teachings in the Book of Proverbs, offers profound insights into the art of decision-making, making it a relevant and invaluable resource for navigating the complexities of the 21st century. This chapter delves even deeper into the practical aspects of seeking wisdom and how it can influence our choices.

Tune your ears to wisdom, and concentrate on understanding. - 2:2

Proverbs 2 underscores the importance of actively seeking wisdom. It encourages us to turn our ear to wisdom and apply our heart to understanding (Proverbs 2:2). In a world where information is abundant but wisdom is often elusive, this chapter reminds us that wisdom must be pursued intentionally. How can this active seeking of wisdom enhance our decision-making in a world saturated with data and choices?

For the Lord grants wisdom! From his mouth come knowledge and understanding. - 2:6

Proverbs 2:6 highlights a crucial aspect of decision-making—the interplay between knowledge and understanding. It states, "For the Lord grants wisdom; from his mouth come knowledge and understanding." This verse invites us to consider how knowledge, the acquisition of information, and understanding, the capacity to comprehend and apply that knowledge, work in tandem to inform our choices. How can we strike a balance between accumulating knowledge and gaining a deeper understanding to make more informed decisions?

He grants a treasure of common sense to the honest. He is a shield to those who walk with integrity. - 2:7

Proverbs 2:7 speaks of the protective role of righteousness in the lives of those who walk in wisdom. Righteousness can shield us from making impulsive or unethical decisions. How might the pursuit of righteousness, or doing what is just and morally upright, serve as a compass for our choices in a world where ethical challenges are prevalent?

Then you will understand what is right, just, and fair, and you will find the right way to go. - 2:9

Proverbs 2:9 describes how wisdom can illuminate our way, enabling us to discern what is right and just. In a world where decision-making often involves navigating ethical gray areas, how does wisdom offer guidance to help us choose the right path?

Wise choices will watch over you. Understanding will keep you safe. - 2:11

Proverbs 2:11 speaks of how discretion will protect us and understanding will guard us. These qualities are crucial for making decisions that preserve our well-being and the well-being of others. How does the cultivation of discretion and understanding enhance our ability to make choices that have a positive impact on our lives and society?

Wisdom will save you from evil people, from those whose words are twisted. These men turn from the right way to walk down dark paths. They take pleasure in doing wrong, and they enjoy the twisted ways of evil. Their actions are crooked, and their ways are wrong. - 2:12-15

The chapter concludes by emphasizing that wisdom will save us from the ways of the wicked and protect us from those who walk in darkness (Proverbs 2:12-15). This speaks to the moral and ethical dimensions of decision-making. How does wisdom guide us in making choices that align with our values and principles, even when faced with conflicting influences?

Proverbs 2 presents a comprehensive guide for decision-making that is deeply rooted in the pursuit of wisdom, knowledge, understanding, and righteousness. It encourages us to actively seek wisdom, balance knowledge and understanding, and integrate the moral and ethical dimensions into our choices. In a rapidly changing and ethically complex world, this chapter reminds us that wisdom can be our guiding light, helping us make decisions that lead to a more meaningful and purposeful life in the 21st century.

Proverbs 3 and Its Relevance to Contemporary Issues

Proverbs 3, a rich source of timeless wisdom, offers valuable insights that are highly relevant to a host of contemporary issues. This chapter serves as a guide for ethical living, decision-making, and personal growth in the complex landscape of the 21st century. Let's explore some of its verses and their applicability to modern challenges:

Never let loyalty and kindness leave you! Tie them around your neck as a reminder. Write them deep within your heart. Then you will find favor with both God and people, and you will earn a good reputation. Trust in the Lord with all your heart; do not depend on your own understanding. - 3:3-4

Proverbs 3:3-4 encourages us to bind kindness and truth around our necks and write them on the tablets of our hearts. This call for kindness and truth is highly relevant in a world grappling with issues of division, intolerance, and misinformation. These verses underscore the importance of cultivating empathy, respect, and integrity as we address contemporary issues involving social harmony and honesty.

Trust in the Lord with all your heart; do not depend on your own understanding. Seek his will in all you do, and he will show you which path to take. - 3:5-6

In a world marked by uncertainty and rapid change, this verse encourages us to have faith and trust in something greater than ourselves. It speaks to the relevance of faith and spirituality in navigating life's challenges and making sense of the unknown.

Don't be impressed with your own wisdom. Instead, fear the Lord and turn away from evil. Then you will have healing for your body and strength for your bones. - 3:7-8

Proverbs 3:7-8 emphasizes the role of wisdom in personal well-being. This message is significant in a society facing modern challenges related to mental health, stress, and self-care. It reminds us that wisdom involves not only external knowledge but also self-awareness and self-care, which are essential for addressing contemporary issues related to well-being.

Honor the Lord with your wealth and with the best part of everything you produce. Then he will fill your barns with grain, and your vats will overflow with good wine. - 3:9-10

Proverbs 3:9-10 advises, "Honor the Lord with your wealth." In a world marked by financial complexities and economic disparities, these verses speak to the importance of responsible financial stewardship, ethical business practices, and generosity. They are highly relevant for addressing contemporary issues of economic inequality and ethical finance.

Joyful is the person who finds wisdom, the one who gains understanding. For wisdom is more profitable than silver, and her wages are better than gold. Wisdom is more precious than rubies; nothing you desire can compare with her. - 3:13-15

Proverbs 3:13-15 extols the value of wisdom, comparing it to precious gems. This passage is pertinent to the modern quest for knowledge and understanding, emphasizing the importance of lifelong learning, critical thinking, and intellectual growth. In a world that places a premium on education and information, the pursuit of wisdom is essential for addressing contemporary issues effectively.

She offers you long life in her right hand, and riches and honor in her left. - 3:16

Proverbs 3:16 promises that wisdom brings long life and prosperity. In the context of modern healthcare, lifestyle choices, and financial planning, this verse underscores the value of making wise choices to ensure longevity and economic well-being.

Do not withhold good from those who deserve it when it's in your power to help them. - 3:27

In a society grappling with issues of social justice, this verse emphasizes the importance of actively contributing to the welfare of others. It encourages us to address contemporary issues of inequality, poverty, and discrimination by taking compassionate and just actions.

Proverbs 3, with its timeless wisdom, continues to be a relevant guide for addressing contemporary issues. It offers insights on trust, kindness, financial stewardship, personal growth, and ethical living. By applying the principles found in this chapter, we can make meaningful contributions to the challenges and opportunities of the 21st century, fostering a more compassionate, just, and purposeful society.

Case Studies and Discussion Questions

Case Study 1: The Intern's Dilemma

Background: Sarah is an intern at a reputable marketing firm. Her supervisor asks her to exaggerate the company's success in their latest ad campaign to attract more clients. She's aware that this might be misleading, but her job is on the line, and she could gain valuable experience.

Proverbs 1 and 2 Connection: Proverbs 1:10-16 cautions against being enticed by sinners and doing wrong. Proverbs 2:6-8 encourages seeking understanding and wisdom to make the right decisions.

Discussion Questions:

What ethical dilemma is Sarah facing, and how does it relate to the wisdom in Proverbs 1 and 2?

How can Sarah apply the guidance from these chapters to make a wise decision?

What values and principles from Proverbs 1 and 2 can guide individuals in navigating ethical challenges in their professional lives?

Case Study 2: Family Feud

Background: The Anderson family is dealing with a long-standing family feud that has caused bitterness and division. The family members are unsure of how to resolve the conflict and reunite.

Proverbs 3 Connection: Proverbs 3:3-4 encourages kindness and truth, which are key to restoring broken relationships. Proverbs 3:5-6 emphasizes trusting in the Lord and leaning not on one's understanding for guidance.

Discussion Questions:

How can the principles of kindness and truth from Proverbs 3 help the Anderson family begin to mend their broken relationships?

In what ways might trusting in the Lord, as advised in Proverbs 3:5-6, help individuals navigate personal conflicts and foster reconciliation?

What can individuals learn from Proverbs 3 about the role of trust, humility, and wisdom in resolving long-standing disputes within families or communities?

Case Study 3: The Business Ethics Dilemma

Background: John, a successful entrepreneur, is faced with a choice. His business partner is encouraging him to cut corners and compromise on product quality to maximize profits. John values integrity and quality but is worried about the impact on the company's financial success.

Proverbs 3 Connection: Proverbs 3:7-8 emphasizes the role of wisdom in personal well-being and decision-making. Proverbs 3:9-10 advises honoring the Lord with wealth and first fruits. This can be seen as a broader principle of ethical financial stewardship.

Discussion Questions:

How does John's ethical dilemma align with the teachings of Proverbs 3:7-8 about the role of wisdom in personal well-being and decision-making?

How might Proverbs 3:9-10 guide John in making choices that honor the Lord with wealth and align with his values of integrity and quality?

What principles of ethical financial stewardship and responsible decision-making can individuals draw from Proverbs 3 in a business context or personal finance?

Note to the Leader for Group Discussion: These case studies and discussion questions provide practical scenarios that resonate with the wisdom found in the first three chapters of Proverbs. They encourage individuals to explore how the timeless principles in Proverbs can be applied to real-life situations, fostering deeper understanding and ethical decision-making.

Chapter 3: The Pursuit of Wisdom

In Chapter 3 of "Proverbs for the 21st Century: A Guide to Wisdom for Young Adults and Adults," we embark on a journey to explore the relentless pursuit of wisdom. This chapter is grounded in the teachings of Proverbs 4, 5, and 6, which are dedicated to unveiling the enduring quest for wisdom and its profound relevance in the complex tapestry of the 21st century.

The pursuit of wisdom is not a passive endeavor but an active and ongoing quest that requires commitment, discernment, and a deep reverence for the invaluable lessons that life offers. Proverbs 4, 5, and 6 serve as a manual for those who seek to navigate the intricacies of life with greater insight and ethical grounding.

In these pages, we will delve into the teachings of Proverbs to uncover the wisdom it imparts, emphasizing that wisdom is not a destination but a path—one that leads to a life enriched with discernment, understanding, and moral integrity. Proverbs 4, 5, and 6 offer a roadmap for how to embark on this journey and continue striving for wisdom throughout our lives.

As we explore the pursuit of wisdom, we will consider the importance of active learning, the value of moral discernment in our decisions, the significance of guarding our hearts and minds, and the consequences of choosing the path of wisdom over folly. Proverbs 4, 5, and 6 not only guide us on this path but also provide the necessary encouragement to persevere.

So, in this chapter, let's open our hearts and minds to the profound wisdom offered by Proverbs, understanding that the pursuit of wisdom is not only a noble endeavor but a transformative one. As we journey through the pages of this chapter, may we find inspiration to embrace wisdom as a lifelong companion and a beacon that illuminates the path toward a more ethical, compassionate, and purposeful life in the modern world.

Proverbs 4 and The Nature of Wisdom

Proverbs 4, a chapter dedicated to the pursuit of wisdom, offers profound insights into the nature of wisdom. This chapter encourages us to grasp the essence of wisdom, appreciate its value, and understand its transformative power. Let's explore the nature of wisdom based on Proverbs 4:

My father taught me, "Take my words to heart. Follow my commands, and you will live. Get wisdom; develop good judgment. Don't forget my words or turn away from them. Don't turn your back on wisdom, for she will protect you. Love her, and she will guard you." - 4:5-7

Proverbs 4:5-7 emphasizes the active pursuit of wisdom, encouraging us to acquire wisdom and understanding. This underlines that wisdom is not a destination but a lifelong journey of learning and self-improvement. It is an ongoing quest to gain knowledge, insight, and moral discernment.

Proverbs 4:6 speaks of wisdom as a guide, and verse 9 describes it as an ornament for our heads and a garland for our necks. This imagery portrays wisdom as a constant companion, guiding us through life's challenges and adorning us with its benefits. It is not an abstract concept but a practical guide that shields us from harm.

Proverbs 4:7 portrays wisdom as a highly valued inheritance, something to be treasured and passed down through the generations. This concept highlights the timeless and enduring nature of wisdom. It is not a fleeting or superficial concept but a valuable legacy that enriches our lives.

The way of the righteous is like the first gleam of dawn, which shines ever brighter until the full light of day. But the way of the wicked is like total darkness. They have no idea what they are stumbling over. - 4:18-19

Proverbs 4:18-19 presents wisdom as the path of the righteous, shining brighter and brighter, while the way of the wicked is darkness. This metaphor conveys the idea that wisdom leads us toward moral clarity and enlightenment. It illuminates our decisions and actions, helping us navigate life's complexities with integrity and purpose.

for they bring life to those who find them, and healing to their whole body. - 4:22

Proverbs 4:22 states that wisdom is life to those who find it and health to one's whole body. This perspective underscores the life-giving and nourishing quality of wisdom. It is not a sterile intellectual pursuit but a source of vitality, well-being, and wholeness for the individual.

Guard your heart above all else, for it determines the course of your life. - 4:23

Proverbs 4:23 instructs us to guard our hearts, for everything we do flows from it. Wisdom, in its nature, encourages us to protect our innermost thoughts, emotions, and intentions. It helps us make choices that align with our values and maintain a pure heart.

In summary, Proverbs 4 portrays wisdom as an invaluable inheritance, a lifelong pursuit, a guiding light, a source of life and health, and a guardian of the heart. The nature of wisdom, as revealed in this chapter, is deeply rooted in its enduring and practical qualities. It is not a distant or unattainable ideal but a tangible, transformative force that enriches our lives, provides moral direction, and empowers us to navigate the complexities of the 21st century with grace and purpose.

Proverbs 5 and How to Seek Wisdom in Today's World

Proverbs 5 offers valuable guidance on seeking wisdom, especially in today's fast-paced and information-saturated world. The chapter primarily focuses on the importance of marital fidelity and the consequences of infidelity, but its principles can be extended to seeking wisdom in various aspects of life. Here's how we can apply the wisdom of Proverbs 5 to our modern context:

Then you will show discernment, and your lips will express what you have learned. - 5:2

Proverbs 5:2 underscores the significance of open and honest communication within a marriage. In a digital age marked by virtual communication and sometimes shallow connections, seeking wisdom involves fostering genuine and transparent interactions with others. Open dialogues can lead to mutual understanding and better decision-making.

For the lips of an immoral woman are as sweet as honey, and her mouth is smoother than oil. But in the end, she is as bitter as poison, as dangerous as a double-edged sword. - 5:3-4

Proverbs 5:3-4 underscores the importance of treating others with respect and integrity. In a society where ethical conduct is sometimes overlooked, seeking wisdom involves adhering to principles of respect, honesty, and moral integrity in all our interactions, whether personal or professional.

For she cares nothing about the path to life. She staggers down a crooked trail and does not realize it. So now, my sons, listen to me. Never stray from what I am about to say. - 5:6-7

Proverbs 5:6-7 emphasizes the importance of prioritizing one's commitments and relationships. In today's world, where distractions and conflicting priorities are abundant, seeking wisdom requires us to identify what truly matters in our personal and professional lives. Prioritizing our values, goals, and relationships can help us make wiser decisions.

Stay away from her! Don't go near the door of her house! If you do, you will lose your honor and will lose to merciless people all you have achieved. - 5:8-9

The chapter encourages setting boundaries and practicing self-discipline in marital relationships. In a world of unlimited digital access and temptations, seeking wisdom means establishing boundaries in all aspects of life, whether it's managing screen time, setting financial limits, or maintaining ethical standards. Self-discipline is essential for making wise choices.

Oh, why didn't I listen to my teachers? Why didn't I pay attention to my instructors? I have come to the brink of utter ruin, and now I must face public disgrace. - 5:13-14

Proverbs 5:13-14 encourages a commitment to personal growth and moral development within a marriage. In the 21st century, seeking wisdom involves a similar commitment to lifelong learning, self-improvement, and ethical growth. It's about continuously seeking knowledge, refining one's character, and adapting to changing circumstances.

Drink water from your own well—share your love only with your wife. - 5:15

In a world of constant distractions and multitasking, Proverbs 5:15 reminds us to stay mindful and present in our relationships. Seeking wisdom today includes practicing mindfulness, which can help us make more deliberate and thoughtful choices in our interactions and decision-making.

An evil man is held captive by his own sins; they are ropes that catch and hold him. He will die for lack of self-control; he will be lost because of his great foolishness. - 5:22-23

Proverbs 5 also highlights the repercussions of unwise choices. In today's world, where instant gratification and impulsive decisions are prevalent, seeking wisdom necessitates a reflective approach. We can learn from the consequences of our past actions and use them as valuable lessons to guide future decisions.

By applying the principles found in Proverbs 5, we can seek wisdom in today's world by prioritizing what truly matters, maintaining open and honest communication, learning from our mistakes, setting boundaries, upholding respect and integrity, committing to personal growth, and staying mindful and present. This wisdom can guide us in making decisions that lead to fulfilling and purposeful lives in the complexities of the 21st century.

Proverbs 6 and Personal Growth Along With Self-Improvement

Proverbs 6 offers profound wisdom that can guide us in our journey of personal growth and self-improvement. This chapter presents valuable insights that are highly relevant to the modern pursuit of self-enhancement. Here's how we can apply the wisdom of Proverbs 6 to cultivate personal growth:

Take a lesson from the ants, you lazybones. Learn from their ways and become wise! Though they have no prince or governor or ruler to make them work, they labor hard all summer, gathering food for the winter. - 6:6-8

Proverbs 6:6-8 draws our attention to the industriousness and self-discipline of ants. They work diligently without external supervision. In the context of personal growth, this verse encourages us to adopt a strong work ethic and self-motivation. We should take responsibility for our development and progress, seeking self-improvement without waiting for external direction.

But you, lazybones, how long will you sleep? When will you wake up? A little extra sleep, a little more slumber, a little folding of the hands to rest—then poverty will pounce on you like a bandit; scarcity will attack you like an armed robber. - 6:9-11

Proverbs 6:9-11 sternly warns against laziness and procrastination, which hinder personal growth. In the modern world, distractions and the allure of instant gratification can lead to procrastination. This verse encourages us to recognize the consequences of such behaviors and emphasizes the importance of taking action and seizing opportunities for self-improvement.

There are six things the Lord hates—no, seven things he detests: haughty eyes, a lying tongue, hands that kill the innocent, a heart that plots evil, feet that race to do wrong, a false witness who pours out lies, a person who sows discord in a family. - 6:16-19

Personal growth is intertwined with moral development and ethical conduct. Proverbs 6 enumerates actions detestable to the Lord, including bearing false witness and stirring up conflict. To foster personal growth, we must cultivate virtues like truthfulness, integrity, and peacemaking. These qualities not only contribute to self-improvement but also nurture harmonious relationships.

My son, obey your father's commandes and don't neglect your mother's instruction. Keep their words always in your heart. Tie them around your neck. When you walk, their counsel will lead you. When you sleep, they will protect you. When you wake up, they will advise you. For their command is a lamp and their instruction a light; their corrective discipline is the way to life. - 6:20-23

Proverbs 6:20-23 reminds us of the guidance and wisdom imparted by parents and mentors. Seeking such guidance is a fundamental element of personal growth. In the 21st century, this includes being open to learning from mentors, peers, and various sources of knowledge, which can significantly contribute to self-improvement.

Excuses might be found for a thief who steals because he is starving. But if he is caught, he must pay back seven times what he stole, even if he has to sell everything in his house. - 6:30-31

These two verses highlight the potential for redemption and reconciliation. In the context of personal growth, it underscores the importance of acknowledging mistakes and seeking opportunities for repentance and self-improvement. Recognizing our errors and making amends is a crucial aspect of growth and moral development.

Incorporating these principles from Proverbs 6 into our lives can foster personal growth and self-improvement. This chapter underscores the importance of a strong work ethic, the avoidance of procrastination, ethical conduct, the value of redemption, and the seeking of wisdom. By embracing these teachings, we can embark on a transformative journey of self-improvement and moral development, becoming better versions of ourselves in the modern world.

Exercises and Reflections

Exercise 1: Prioritizing Values

Reflection: Proverbs 4:7 advises us to get wisdom and develop good judgment. Reflect on your core values and priorities. What aspects of your life could benefit from a deeper understanding? Write down the values you hold most dear and identify one area where you can invest in gaining greater wisdom and understanding to align with these values.

Exercise 2: Setting Boundaries

Reflection: Proverbs 5:8-9 encourages setting boundaries to avoid temptation and make wise choices. Think about an area in your life where you struggle with temptation or impulsive decisions. What boundaries can you set to protect yourself from these temptations? Reflect on how implementing these boundaries can lead to personal growth and self-improvement.

Exercise 3: Learning from Consequences

Reflection: Proverbs 6:23 states, "For their command is a lamp and their instruction a light; their corrective discipline is the way to life." Consider a recent mistake or error in judgment you've made. Reflect on the consequences of that action. What lessons can you draw from this experience, and how can you apply these lessons to avoid repeating the same mistake in the future?

Exercise 4: Pursuing Wisdom Actively

Reflection: Proverbs 4:7 encourages us to "get wisdom." In what areas of your life do you actively seek wisdom and understanding? Are there any aspects where you've been passive or neglectful in seeking knowledge? Reflect on how you can become more intentional in your pursuit of wisdom and how it can contribute to your personal growth and self-improvement.

Exercise 5: Commitment to Ethical Conduct

Reflection: Proverbs 6:16-19 lists actions detestable to the Lord, including a lying tongue and stirring up conflict. Reflect on your conduct in relationships and community. Have you engaged in any actions or behaviors that align with these detestable actions? How can you commit to a more ethical and virtuous way of interacting with others, fostering personal growth in your character?

Exercise 6: Seeking Guidance

Reflection: Proverbs 4:20-22 encourages us to listen to the teachings of our parents and keep them close. Reflect on the guidance you've received from parents, mentors, or wise individuals in your life. How have their teachings influenced your decisions and actions? In what ways can you be more receptive to their wisdom and guidance to promote your personal growth and self-improvement?

Note to Leader for Group Discussion: These exercises and reflections based on Proverbs 4, 5, and 6 provide a framework for self-examination and personal development. They encourage you to prioritize values, set boundaries, learn from consequences, actively pursue wisdom, commit to ethical conduct, and seek guidance. By engaging in these exercises and deep reflections, you can embark on a journey of self-improvement and personal growth in alignment with the wisdom found in these chapters.

Chapter 4: Relationships and Communication

Welcome to Chapter 4 of "Proverbs for the 21st Century: A Guide to Wisdom for Young Adults and Adults." This chapter delves into the timeless wisdom found in Proverbs 6 to 9, exploring the intricate dynamics of relationships and the art of effective communication. These chapters provide invaluable insights into building meaningful connections, navigating the complexities of human interactions, and fostering a foundation of wisdom in our relationships.

As we embark on this journey through Proverbs 6 to 9, we will encounter verses that address the essence of friendship, the consequences of destructive behaviors, the wisdom of listening, and the importance of honest communication. This section of Proverbs offers a wealth of guidance on how to cultivate healthy relationships and communicate with wisdom and discernment.

In a world where relationships can be both a source of profound fulfillment and significant challenges, the teachings of Proverbs 6 to 9 remain remarkably relevant. The principles contained within these chapters provide a roadmap for fostering positive connections, resolving conflicts, and establishing communication patterns that align with the values of wisdom and understanding.

Throughout this chapter, we will reflect on the practical wisdom of Proverbs, exploring how it can be applied to our contemporary relationships. From friendships and family connections to professional interactions, the timeless principles found in Proverbs 6 to 9 offer profound insights into the dynamics of human connection and the role of communication in nurturing healthy, fulfilling relationships.

So, let us delve into the wisdom of Proverbs and uncover the pearls of insight that will guide us in building strong, meaningful relationships and communicating with grace, empathy, and wisdom in the intricate tapestry of the 21st century.

Wisdom in Relationships: Insights from Proverbs 6 and 7

The Book of Proverbs provides profound insights into the nature of wisdom and its crucial role in fostering healthy connections. Proverbs 6 and the first half of Proverbs 7 offer a wealth of wisdom specifically tailored to guide us in the realm of relationships.

My child, if you have put up security for a friend's debt or agreed to guarantee the debt of a stranger—if you have trapped yourself by your agreement and are caught by what you said—follow my advice and save yourself, for you have placed yourself at your friend's mercy. Now swallow your pride; go and beg to have your name erased. - 6:1-3

We are advised against becoming entangled in financial agreements with others. While the context may be financial, the underlying principle speaks to the importance of careful commitment in all aspects of relationships. Wisdom calls us to consider the implications of our commitments and to enter into them thoughtfully, whether they are financial, emotional, or relational.

Take a lesson from the ants, you lazybones. Learn from their ways and become wise! Though they have no prince or governor or ruler to make them work, they labor hard all summer, gathering food for the winter. But you, lazybones, how long will you sleep? When will you wake up? A little extra sleep, a little more slumber, a little folding of the hands to rest-then poverty will pounce on you like a bandit; scarcity will attack you like an armed robber. - 6:6-11

Proverbs paints a vivid picture of the consequences of laziness and discord. In relationships, this echoes the profound truth that negligence and strife can lead to severe repercussions. Wisdom prompts us to actively contribute to the well-being of our relationships, fostering an environment of harmony and mutual respect.

My son, obey your father's commandes, and don't neglect your mother's instruction. Keep their words always in your heart. Tie them around your neck. When you walk, their counsel will lead you.

When you sleep, they will protect you. When you wake up, they will advise you. For their command is a lamp and their instruction a light; their corrective discipline is the way to life. - 6:20-23

These verses portray wisdom as a guardian, likening it to a sister and an understanding kinsman. In relationships, wisdom plays a protective role, guiding us away from detrimental connections and encouraging us to seek those that contribute positively to our lives.

It will keep you from the immoral woman, from the smooth tongue of a promiscuous woman. Don't lust for her beauty. Don't let her coy glances seduce you. For a prostitute will bring you to poverty, but sleeping with another man's wife will cost you your life. Can a man scoop a flame into his lap and not have his clothes catch on fire? Can he walk on hot coals and not blister his feet? So it is with the man who sleeps with another man's wife. He who embraces her will not go unpunished. - 6:24-29

Vigilance against temptation is illuminated by the dangers of falling into the allure of forbidden relationships. The narrative of the adulterous woman serves as a metaphor for destructive temptations. Wisdom encourages vigilance, cautioning against the seduction of harmful influences in relationships.

Love wisdom like a sister; make insight a beloved member of your family. Let them protect you from an affair with an immoral woman, from listening to the flattery of a promiscuous woman. - 6:4-5

The role of wisdom as a guardian underscores the protective role of wisdom. It is likened to a sister and an understanding kinsman who guards against the seduction of harmful influences. In relationships, wisdom acts as a guardian, guiding us away from detrimental connections and encouraging us to seek those that contribute positively to our lives.

I saw some naive young men, and one in particular who lacked common sense. He was crossing the street near the house of an immoral woman, strolling down the path by her house. It was at twilight, in the evening, as deep darkness fell. - 6:7-9

The adulterous woman introduces the cautionary tale of the young man and the adulterous woman. This narrative serves as a metaphor for the allure of destructive temptations in relationships. Wisdom, in this context, prompts us to be vigilant and discerning, recognizing the potential harm that enticing but unhealthy relationships can bring.

In summary, Proverbs 6 and the first half of Proverbs 7 offer a comprehensive guide to the application of wisdom in relationships. From the importance of careful commitment and the consequences of discord to the vigilant discernment needed to avoid destructive influences, these passages underscore the transformative power of wisdom in fostering positive, enriching connections. As we navigate the intricate landscape of human relationships, the wisdom found in Proverbs serves as a guiding light, offering timeless principles for building and sustaining healthy, meaningful connections.

Effective Communication: Wisdom from Proverbs 7 and 8

In the pursuit of wisdom, the latter part of Proverbs 7 and the entirety of Proverbs 8 offer profound insights into the art of effective communication. These chapters guide us in navigating conversations, imparting wisdom, and fostering understanding in our interactions with others.

So she seduced him with her pretty speech and enticed him with her flattery. He followed her at once, like an ox going to the slaughter. He was like a stag caught in a trap, awaiting the arrow that would pierce its heart. He was like a bird flying into a snare, little knowing it would cost him his life. - 7:21-23

The craft of persuasive communication vividly depicts the persuasive words of the adulterous woman. While the context is cautionary, it reveals the power of effective communication. Wisdom, in relationships and beyond, involves recognizing the impact of words and striving to communicate with sincerity and clarity.

Listen as Wisdom calls out! Hear as understanding raises her voice! On the hilltop along the road, she takes her stand at the crossroads. By the gates at the entrance to the town, on the road leading in, she cries aloud, "I call to you, to all of you! I raise my voice to all people. You simple people, use good judgment. You foolish people, show some understanding. - 8:1-5

The call of Wisdom in public squares introduces Wisdom personified, calling out in the public squares and at the city gates. This imagery emphasizes the accessibility of wisdom and its constant invitation to be heard. Effective communication, as depicted here, involves making one's message accessible and engaging, reaching people where they are.

Listen to me! For I have important things to tell you. Everything I say is right, for I speak the truth and detest every kind of deception. My advice is wholesome. There is nothing devious or crooked in it. My words are plain to anyone with understanding, clear to those with knowledge. - 8:6-9

Wisdom's speech as right and true portrays the speech of Wisdom as right, true, and devoid of wickedness. In the realm of effective communication, these qualities are foundational. Wisdom calls us to communicate honestly, avoiding deceit and cultivating a reputation for reliability in our words.

Choose my instruction rather than silver, and knowledge rather than pure gold. For wisdom is far more valuable than rubies. Nothing you desire can compare with it. - 8:10-11

The value of understanding underscores the immeasurable value of wisdom and understanding, surpassing the most precious materials. Effective communication requires an understanding of the subject matter and the audience. It involves conveying messages that resonate with the listener's values and experiences.

And so, my children, listen to me, for all who follow my ways are joyful. Listen to my instruction and be wise. Don't ignore it. Joyful are those who listen to me, watching for me daily at my gates, waiting for me outside my home! - 8:32-34

The blessings of those who listen express the blessings bestowed upon those who listen to Wisdom. Effective communication is a two-way street; it involves not only articulating thoughts clearly but also actively listening to others. Wisdom encourages a receptive attitude, fostering an environment where understanding can flourish.

For whoever finds me finds life and receives favor from the Lord. But those who miss me injure themselves. All who hate me love death. - 8:35-36

The joy of those who heed Wisdom's instruction describes the joy experienced by those who heed Wisdom's instruction. Effective communication leads to positive outcomes and shared understanding. When we communicate with wisdom, our words have the potential to bring joy, enlightenment, and a sense of unity to those who receive them.

In summary, the latter part of Proverbs 7 and the entirety of Proverbs 8 illuminate the principles of effective communication. From recognizing the power of persuasive words and the accessibility of wisdom to understanding the immeasurable value of clear, honest speech, these chapters guide us in cultivating communication that builds bridges, fosters understanding, and brings joy to our interactions. In the intricate tapestry of relationships and the broader spheres of life, the wisdom found in Proverbs 7 and 8 beckons us to communicate with thoughtfulness, clarity, and a deep commitment to truth.

Building Healthy Connections: Wisdom from Proverbs 9

Proverbs 9 serves as a beacon of wisdom, offering timeless insights into the art of building and sustaining healthy connections. In this chapter, wisdom is personified as a gracious hostess, inviting us to partake in the feast of understanding and discernment. Let's explore the profound guidance Proverbs 9 provides for cultivating relationships that stand the test of time.

Wisdom has built her house; she has carved its seven columns. She has prepared a great banquet, mixed the wines, and set the table. She has sent her servants to invite everyone to come. She calls out from the heights overlooking the city. "Come in with me," she urges the simple. To those who lack good judgment, she says, "Come, eat my food, and drink the wine I have mixed. Leave your simple ways behind, and begin to live; learn to use good judgment." - 9:1-6

The invitation to Wisdom's feast presents Wisdom as a gracious hostess who has built her house and prepared a feast. Building healthy connections begins with an invitation, an openness to share and partake in the wisdom of others. Just as Wisdom extends an invitation, we are encouraged to approach relationships with a welcoming spirit, creating spaces where understanding and insight can be shared.

Anyone who rebukes a mocker will get an insult in return. Anyone who corrects the wicked will get hurt. So don't bother correcting mockers; they will only hate you. But correct the wise, and they will love you. Instruct the wise, and they will be even wiser. Teach the righteous, and they will learn even more. - 9:7-9

Correcting the mocker warns against correcting a mocker, as it may invite insults. Building healthy connections requires discernment in our interactions. Not every connection is meant to be deep or transformative. Wisdom encourages us to invest our time and energy in relationships where mutual respect and a willingness to learn from one another exist.

Fear of the Lord is the foundation of wisdom. Knowledge of the Holy One results in good judgment. Wisdom will multiply your days and add years to your life. If you become wise, you will be the one to benefit. If you scorn wisdom, you will be the one to suffer. - 9:10-12

The essence of fearing the Lord emphasizes that the fear of the Lord is the beginning of wisdom. Building healthy connections is rooted in reverence—respecting the divine spark within each person. This foundational principle encourages us to approach relationships with a sense of awe, recognizing the inherent worth and potential for growth in others.

The promise of long life assures that through wisdom your days will be many, and years will be added to your life. Building and maintaining healthy connections contribute to a fulfilling and extended life. In relationships, the positive impact of wisdom ripples through shared experiences, creating a supportive network that enriches the journey of life.

Choosing the way of insight contrasts the wise and the mocker, emphasizing the consequences of choosing the way of insight versus the way of arrogance. Healthy connections are built on a foundation of mutual respect and a shared commitment to personal and collective growth. Wisdom calls us to choose humility over pride, creating spaces where individuals can learn from one another.

In conclusion, Proverbs 9 provides a profound blueprint for building and nurturing healthy connections. By extending invitations of understanding, embracing humility, discerning wisely, choosing the path of insight, and fostering an environment of mutual respect, we participate in the timeless feast of wisdom. As we navigate the intricate dynamics of relationships, the wisdom found in Proverbs 9 calls us to build connections that not only endure the tests of time but also contribute to a shared journey of understanding, growth, and fulfillment.

Role Play and Group Activities

As we journey through Proverbs 6 to 9, a rich tapestry of wisdom unfolds, guiding us through the complexities of relationships, effective communication, and the art of building healthy connections. This reflective page invites you to delve deeper into the wisdom found in these chapters through role-play and group activities. Let's engage in exercises that not only help internalize these teachings but also foster meaningful discussions and shared insights.

Role Play: A Wisdom-Infused Conversation Objective: To embody the principles of effective communication from Proverbs 7 and 8 through role-play.

Instructions :

Form pairs or small groups.

Assign roles, such as the persuader (reflecting Proverbs 7:21-23) and the listener.

The persuader should attempt to convey a message persuasively, while the listener actively practices discernment and cautious listening.

After the role-play, discuss the experience. What elements of effective communication did you observe? How did discernment play a role?

Group Activity: Building the House of Wisdom Objective: To visually represent the concept of building a foundation of wisdom in relationships inspired by Proverbs 9:1-6.

Instructions :

Provide each participant with art supplies (paper, markers, glue, scissors, etc.).

Ask each participant to draw or construct a symbolic representation of a house, incorporating elements that signify wisdom in relationships.

Encourage creativity and diversity in the interpretations.

Assemble the individual creations into a collective display, representing a community of wisdom-built houses.

Facilitate a discussion: How did the creative process reflect the principles of building healthy connections? What symbols did participants choose to represent wisdom?

Role Play: The Banquet of Understanding Objective: To embody the concept of inviting others to partake in the feast of wisdom, as seen in Proverbs 9:1-6.

Instructions :

Form groups, designating one person as the host/hostess and the rest as guests.

The host/hostess should create an imaginary scenario where they are hosting a banquet of understanding.

Each guest, in turn, expresses how they contribute to the banquet through sharing wisdom, experiences, or insights.

After the role-play, discuss the experience. How did the exercise illustrate the concept of inviting others to partake in the feast of wisdom? How did it foster a sense of shared understanding and connection?

Group Reflection: Wisdom in Action Objective: To collectively reflect on how the wisdom from Proverbs 6 to 9 can be applied in daily life.

Instructions :

Facilitate a group discussion on key takeaways from the chapters.

Ask participants to share personal experiences where they have applied or witnessed the principles of wisdom discussed in these chapters.

Encourage participants to brainstorm ways they can incorporate these teachings into their everyday interactions.

Create a collective commitment board where participants pledge to practice specific aspects of wisdom in their lives.

Note to Leader for Group Discussion: By engaging in these role-play and group activities, we aim to internalize the wisdom found in Proverbs 6 to 9, fostering a deeper understanding of effective communication, building healthy connections, and embodying the principles of wisdom in our daily lives. As we reflect and share insights, may this experience be a stepping stone towards a more intentional and wisdom-infused journey in the intricate landscape of relationships.

Chapter 5: Work, Wealth, and Success

Welcome to Chapter 5 of "Proverbs for the 21st Century: A Guide to Wisdom for Young Adults and Adults." In this chapter, we embark on an exploration of the timeless wisdom found in Proverbs, specifically focusing on the intricate interplay of work, wealth, and success. Drawing insights from chapters 10 to 13, these verses offer profound guidance on the principles governing our professional lives, financial decisions, and the pursuit of a meaningful and prosperous existence.

In a world where the dynamics of work, wealth, and success are ever-evolving, the wisdom encapsulated in Proverbs serves as a beacon, guiding navigating the complexities of our careers and financial landscapes. Whether you're in the early stages of your professional journey or are a seasoned veteran, these teachings offer practical and ethical principles that resonate across diverse career paths and financial endeavors.

As we delve into the verses of Proverbs 10 to 13, our focus will be on understanding the importance of diligence, the ethical foundations of financial prosperity, and the true measures of success. This chapter aims to be a compass, guiding you through the choices and challenges that arise in your pursuit of a fulfilling and prosperous life.

So, let us journey together into the wisdom of Proverbs chapters 10 to 13, uncovering the nuggets of truth that will inspire and guide us in our professional endeavors, financial decisions, and the quest for success in the unique landscape of the 21st century.

Proverbs on Prosperity and Success

The Book of Proverbs provides timeless wisdom, illuminating the path to prosperity and success. Chapters 10 and 11 offer profound insights into the principles that govern our pursuit of abundance and achievement. Let's explore these verses, where nuggets of truth guide us through the landscape of prosperity.

Lazy people are soon poor; hard workers get rich. - 10:4

The foundational principle of diligence is a cornerstone in the pursuit of prosperity. This proverb urges us to engage in our work with commitment and industriousness, recognizing that the road to success is often paved with hard work.

The earnings of the godly enhance their lives, but evil people squander their money on sin. - 10:16

This proverb draws a connection between righteousness and positive outcomes. It suggests that ethical conduct, integrity, and righteousness contribute to a prosperous life, emphasizing that success is not merely financial but encompasses the richness of a meaningful existence.

Too much talk leads to sin. Be sensible and keep your mouth shut. - 10:19

Success is often intertwined with wise communication. This proverb encourages us to be discerning in our speech, highlighting that prosperity can be influenced by the thoughtful use of words, emphasizing quality over quantity.

Honesty guides good people; dishonesty destroys treacherous people. - 11:3

Success is not just about reaching a destination but navigating the journey with integrity. This verse underscores that a righteous and principled approach acts as a guide, ensuring a sustainable and honorable legacy.

Without wise leadership, a nation falls; there is safety in having many advisers. - 11:14

Success often involves seeking counsel and learning from the wisdom of others. This proverb underscores the value of diverse perspectives and the importance of humility in our pursuit of prosperity.

The generous will prosper; those who refresh others will themselves be refreshed. - 11:25

Prosperity is not solely about personal gain but extends to how we uplift and support those around us. This proverb emphasizes the reciprocal nature of generosity, suggesting that success is enriched when shared with others.

Proverbs 10 and the beginning of 11 provide a roadmap for navigating prosperity and success. From the diligence that shapes our endeavors to the ethical foundations that guide our actions, these verses illuminate a holistic understanding of success—one that encompasses not only financial prosperity but also righteousness, wise communication, generosity, and the importance of seeking guidance. As we integrate these proverbs into our lives, may they serve as guiding lights on our journey toward a truly prosperous and meaningful existence.

Ethical Business and Financial Practices

In the realm of business and finance, the Book of Proverbs serves as a timeless guide, offering insights into ethical conduct, financial prudence, and the foundations of prosperity. Proverbs 12, in particular, provides a wealth of wisdom that resonates with the principles of ethical business practices. Let's explore these verses and glean insights into fostering integrity and wisdom in the world of commerce.

Wickedness never brings stability, but the godly have deep roots. - 12:3

Ethical business practices contribute to long-term stability. This proverb suggests that righteousness and integrity form a foundation that withstands the tests of time, fostering a sustainable and resilient business environment.

Fools think their own way is right, but the wise listen to others. - 12:15

Ethical business leaders value wise counsel. This proverb underscores the importance of humility in decision-making, acknowledging that seeking and heeding advice contributes to sound and ethical business practices.

An honest witness tells the truth; a false witness tells lies. - 12:17

The essence of ethical business lies in the commitment to honesty. This proverb emphasizes the importance of truthful testimony, highlighting that integrity forms the bedrock of trustworthy business dealings.

Some people make cutting remarks, but the words of the wise bring healing. - 12:18

In the business world, communication holds immense power. Ethical practices encompass thoughtful and considerate speech, recognizing that words can impact relationships, reputation, and overall business success.

Truthful words stand the test of time, but lies are soon exposed. - 12:19

Ethical business practices reject deceit, recognizing that the consequences of dishonesty may be short-lived. This proverb encourages a commitment to truthfulness, acknowledging that enduring success is built on a foundation of trust.

Work hard and become a leader; be lazy and become a slave. - 12:24

Ethical business practices involve a diligent and committed approach to work. This proverb underscores that success is often bestowed upon those who engage in their endeavors with industry and dedication.

Proverbs 12 serves as a guide for ethical business and financial practices. From the importance of honesty and diligence to the impact of thoughtful speech and the enduring consequences of deceit, these verses offer a comprehensive understanding of the principles that underpin ethical conduct in the business world. As we integrate these proverbs into our professional lives, may they inspire us to cultivate businesses that thrive not only in financial prosperity but, more importantly, in integrity, trust, and enduring success.

Balancing Work and Life

In the hustle and bustle of daily life, achieving a harmonious balance between work and personal well-being is a universal challenge. The Book of Proverbs, a treasury of timeless wisdom, provides insights that resonate with the principles of maintaining equilibrium between professional responsibilities and a fulfilling life. Proverbs 13, in particular, offers profound guidance on finding this balance. Let's explore these verses and extract wisdom on harmonizing work and life.

Those who control their tongue will have a long life; opening your mouth can ruin everything. - 13:3

In the quest for balance, mindful communication is crucial. This proverb emphasizes the impact of words on personal well-being, advocating for thoughtful speech to nurture both professional and personal relationships.

Lazy people want much but get little, but those who work hard will prosper. - 13:4

Balancing work and life involve diligence. This proverb underscores that a diligent and focused approach to work not only satisfies professional ambitions but also creates room for a more fulfilling personal life.

Some who are poor pretend to be rich; others who are rich pretend to be poor. - 13:7

Balancing work and life is not solely about accumulating wealth. This proverb encourages reflection on the true measure of wealth, emphasizing contentment and the recognition that a rich life extends beyond material success.

The life of the godly is full of light and joy, but the light of the wicked will be snuffed out. - 13:9

Balancing work and life requires righteous living. This proverb metaphorically suggests that maintaining a balance between professional responsibilities and personal well-being is facilitated by living with integrity and ethical conduct.

Pride leads to conflict; those who take advice are wise. - 13:10

Achieving balance involves seeking wise counsel. This proverb highlights the importance of humility and the wisdom gained through seeking advice, both in professional and personal decision-making.

The instruction of the wise is like a life-giving fountain; those who accept it avoid the snares of death. - 13:14

Proverbs 13 provides a roadmap for balancing work and life. From the diligence that satisfies professional desires to the recognition of true wealth and the power of thoughtful communication, these verses offer a holistic understanding of achieving equilibrium. As we integrate these proverbs into our daily lives, may they inspire us to pursue success with diligence, appreciate the wealth of contentment, and navigate the delicate dance between work and life with wisdom and grace.

Practical Exercises

Embracing the wisdom found in Proverbs 10-13 involves more than mere understanding; it calls for practical application in our daily lives. Here are some exercises inspired by these proverbs, designed to help you integrate their timeless teachings into your routines:

Wisdom in Communication: Exercise: Choose a day to practice mindful communication. Before speaking, pause and consider the impact of your words. Strive to be intentional, avoiding rash or harmful speech. Reflect in the evening on your experiences and the influence of thoughtful communication on your interactions.

Journaling for Diligence: Exercise: Maintain a diligence journal for a week. Record your daily tasks, noting moments where diligence played a role in your work or personal life. Identify patterns, challenges, and areas for improvement. Share your reflections with a friend or mentor to gain additional insights.

Wealth Beyond Money: Exercise: Create a "Wealth Beyond Money" vision board. Use images, quotes, and symbols that represent aspects of life you consider truly valuable—relationships, personal growth, experiences, etc. Display this board in a prominent place to serve as a daily reminder of your broader definition of wealth.

Wealth Beyond Money: Exercise: Create a "Wealth Beyond Money" vision board. Use images, quotes, and symbols that represent aspects of life you consider truly valuable—relationships, personal growth, experiences, etc. Display this board in a prominent place to serve as a daily reminder of your broader definition of wealth.

Gratitude Practice: Exercise: Start a gratitude journal focusing on both personal and professional aspects of your life. Each day, jot down three things you're grateful for. This exercise cultivates an attitude of contentment and aligns with the wisdom of appreciating the richness of life beyond material success.

Personal Integrity Audit: Exercise: Conduct a personal integrity audit. Reflect on recent decisions and actions, considering how they align with your values. Identify any areas where you feel you could improve in maintaining personal integrity. Develop a plan to address these areas and track your progress over time.

Mindful Decision-Making: Exercise: Before making a significant decision, practice mindfulness. Take a few moments to center yourself, considering the potential impact of your choices on both professional and personal aspects of your life. This exercise promotes intentional decision-making aligned with wisdom.

Generosity Challenge: Exercise: Engage in a generosity challenge. Identify one way you can be generous each day, whether through acts of kindness, sharing knowledge, or supporting others. Reflect on the impact of generosity on your well-being and the well-being of those around you.

Balanced Time Tracker: Exercise: Keep a time tracker for a week, noting how you spend your time in various aspects of life—work, relationships, personal growth, leisure, etc. Analyze the data to identify any imbalances. Adjust your schedule to prioritize neglected areas, fostering a more balanced and fulfilling life.

10. Weekly Reflection on Growth: Exercise: Every week, set aside time for a personal and professional reflection. Consider the areas where you've grown, challenges you've faced, and lessons learned. Use this reflection to refine your goals and aspirations, ensuring a continuous journey toward wisdom and personal6 development.

Note to Leader for Group Discussion: These practical exercises aim to transform the wisdom found in Proverbs 10-13 into actionable steps for personal and professional growth. Embrace these exercises with an open heart and a commitment to applying the teachings of Proverbs in your daily life

Chapter 6: The Fear of the Lord

Embarking on a journey through Proverbs 14-17, we delve into a theme that resonates at the core of wisdom literature: the fear of the Lord. This profound concept transcends mere trepidation; it encapsulates reverence, awe, and a deep-seated understanding of our relationship with the Divine. In these chapters, the fear of the Lord serves as a guiding principle, shaping not only our spiritual connection but also influencing the choices we make in our daily lives.

The fear of the Lord, as depicted in Proverbs 14-17, extends beyond a religious or theological concept; it permeates the fabric of human existence, offering insights into how we navigate relationships, make decisions, and cultivate character. As we explore these verses, we will uncover the multifaceted nature of the fear of the Lord—a concept that intertwines with wisdom, righteousness, and the pursuit of a life that aligns with divine principles.

Proverbs, often referred to as the book of practical wisdom, implores us to consider the fear of the Lord as the beginning of knowledge and wisdom. In a world filled with competing values and ideologies, these chapters beckon us to reflect on the significance of acknowledging a higher power, seeking a moral compass that transcends the temporal, and understanding the transformative power of living in awe of the Divine.

So, let us embark on this exploration of the fear of the Lord in Proverbs 14-17, drawing from the rich tapestry of verses that illuminate the path toward true wisdom, righteous living, and a profound connection with the eternal. May these insights inspire us to approach life with humility, reverence, and a deep awareness of the divine presence that guides our steps.

Understanding the Fear of the Lord

Embarking on a journey through Proverbs 14-19, we delve into a theme that echoes with profound significance—the fear of the Lord. As we traverse through these chapters, the concept unfolds as a thread weaving through the fabric of wisdom literature, inviting us to a deeper understanding of reverence, awe, and a transformative connection with the Divine.

Those who follow the right path fear the Lord; those who take the wrong path despise him. - 14:2

As portrayed here, the fear of the Lord is intrinsically linked to upright living. It inspires a reverence that manifests in a commitment to righteousness, guiding our actions and choices along a moral path.

Fear of the Lord is a life-giving fountain; it offers escape from the snares of death. - 14:27

Here, the fear of the Lord is likened to a fountain, a source of vitality that redirects us from the entanglements of destructive paths. It symbolizes a life-giving force that emanates from a reverential connection with the divine.

Better to have little, with fear for the Lord, than to have great treasure and inner turmoil. - 15:16

The fear of the Lord is presented as a guardian against the restlessness that can accompany material pursuits. It encourages contentment, recognizing the enduring value of a life grounded in reverence.

If you listen to constructive criticism, you will be at home among the wise. - 15:31

The fear of the Lord fosters an openness to correction, recognizing that wisdom often comes through guidance and a willingness to learn.

Fear of the Lord teaches wisdom; humility precedes honor. - 15:33

The fear of the Lord is portrayed as a precursor to wisdom, emphasizing the inseparable connection between humility and honor. It beckons us to approach life with a teachable spirit, recognizing the divine source of true wisdom. It also emphasizes humility as a cornerstone of the fear of the Lord. The interplay between humility and honor signifies that acknowledging the divine order of things fosters an attitude of humility, paving the way for the reception of honor that is aligned with righteous living.

We can make our plans, but the Lord determines our steps. - 16:9

Here, the fear of the Lord is unveiled in the acknowledgment that, while we chart our paths, a higher authority shapes our steps. It calls for trust, surrender, and a recognition of the divine order guiding our endeavors.

A cheerful heart is good medicine, but a broken spirit saps a person's strength. - 17:22

In the context of the fear of the Lord, this verse suggests that a joyful heart is a result of a reverential connection. It becomes a healing balm that soothes the spirit, emphasizing that true joy emanates from a heart attuned to the Divine.

The name of the Lord is a strong fortress; the godly run to him and are safe. - 18:10

This verse signifies that reverence serves as a sanctuary. It is not a place of fear but a fortified refuge where the righteous find safety. The fear of the Lord becomes a haven in times of trouble.

The tongue can bring death or life; those who love to talk will reap the consequences. - 18:21

In the context of the fear of the Lord, this verse suggests that a reverential attitude influences our speech. It becomes a recognition that our words have the power of life when rooted in divine reverence, fostering positive and life-giving communication.

Fear of the Lord leads to life, bringing security and protection from harm. - 19:23

This verse becomes a culmination of our exploration, illustrating that the fear of the Lord is not a burden but a source of life and contentment. It suggests that, in reverential living, one finds a sanctuary untouched by the troubles that may beset the world.

In summary, Proverbs 14-19 unfolds a nuanced and comprehensive understanding of the fear of the Lord—a theme that transcends mere trepidation and becomes a transformative force shaping wisdom, humility, joy, and a life marked by divine contentment. As we immerse ourselves in these chapters, may the fear of the Lord illuminate our paths, guide our steps, and invite us into a profound and life-giving connection with the Divine.

Implications for Faith and Spirituality

In the poetic verses of Proverbs 20 and 21, a rich tapestry of wisdom unfolds, offering profound insights into the realms of faith and spirituality. As we journey through these chapters, let us unravel the implications for a life steeped in faith—a life that acknowledges the divine, seeks wisdom, and navigates the complexities of human existence with a heart aligned with spiritual principles.

Wise words are more valuable than much gold and many rubies. - 20:15

Spirituality lies in recognizing the rarity and preciousness of wisdom. It prompts a pursuit of knowledge and understanding as a spiritual virtue—a quest for insights that align with divine principles.

Don't say, "I will get even for this wrong." Wait for the Lord to handle the matter. - 20:22

In matters of faith, this verse suggests a trust in divine justice—a belief that wrongs will be made right in the overarching plan of the Lord. It calls for patience, forgiveness, and a relinquishing of the desire for personal retribution.

The Lord directs our steps, so why try to understand everything along the way? - 20:24

In these words, we find an implication for faith that suggests an acknowledgment of divine guidance in our life's journey. It encourages a humble surrender, recognizing that understanding our path requires trust in the divine order.

The Lord's light penetrates the human spirit, exposing every hidden motive. - 20:27

The implication for spirituality is found in the recognition that our innermost being, illuminated by the divine, becomes a sacred space. It prompts a focus on the integrity of the heart in worship—a sincere connection with the divine that emanates from the depths of our spirit.

People may be right in their own eyes, but the Lord examines their heart. - 21:2

The implication for spirituality lies in the alignment of the heart with divine principles. It prompts self-reflection and a commitment to cultivate a heart that resonates with righteousness and seeks to embody the values cherished by the Lord.

The Lord is more pleased when we do what is right and just than when we offer him sacrifices. - 21:3

This verse becomes a guiding light for spirituality, emphasizing that the essence of our spiritual practices lies in righteous living. It calls for actions that reflect justice, kindness, and a commitment to ethical principles.

In summary, Proverbs 20 and 21 offer profound implications for faith and spirituality. They beckon us to acknowledge divine guidance, cultivate righteousness, commit our plans to the Lord, and recognize the rare jewel of wisdom. As we immerse ourselves in these verses, may our faith be deepened, our spiritual practices be enriched, and our hearts be aligned with the timeless principles illuminated by the wisdom of Proverbs.

Worship and Reverence

In the verses of Proverbs 22 and 23, a symphony of wisdom unfolds, offering profound insights into the realms of worship and reverence. As we navigate through these chapters, let us unravel the implications for a life steeped in worship—a life that acknowledges the divine, embraces reverence, and seeks wisdom for navigating the intricate tapestry of human existence.

Choose a good reputation over great riches; being held in high esteem is better than silver or gold. - 22:1

In the context of worship, this verse becomes an invitation to recognize the intrinsic value of a good name—a reputation cultivated through righteous living and aligned with divine principles. It prompts us to approach life with integrity as an act of worship.

True humility and fear of the Lord lead to riches, honor, and long life. - 22:4

In matters of reverence and worship, this verse underscores the connection between humility and the fear of the Lord. It suggests that true worship involves approaching the Divine with a humble heart, seeking wisdom, and reaping the rich rewards of honor and life.

Direct your children onto the right path, and when they are older, they will not leave it. - 22:6

In the context of worship and reverence, this verse emphasizes the role of teaching and training in righteousness. It invites us to instill divine principles in the hearts of the next generation, fostering a legacy of reverence and worship.

Blessed are those who are generous, because they feed the poor. - 22:9

This verse suggests that true worship extends beyond rituals to encompass acts of generosity and compassion. It prompts us to view our resources as opportunities for worship—blessing others and, in turn, experiencing divine blessings.

Don't rob the poor just because you can, or exploit the needy in court. For the Lord is their defender. He will ruin anyone who ruins them. - 22:22-23

This passage underscores the divine concern for justice and the vulnerable. It prompts us to approach others with fairness and empathy, recognizing that our treatment of others is an aspect of our worshipful response to the Lord.

While dining with a ruler, pay attention to what is put before you. If you are a big eater, put a knife to your throat; don't desire all the delicacies, for he might be trying to trick you. - 23:1-3

In the context of worship and reverence, these verses prompt us to approach the banquet of life with moderation and discernment. They invite us to recognize the sacredness of our bodies and lives as vessels for worship, prompting gratitude and mindfulness in our daily choices.

Commit yourself to instruction; listen carefully to words of knowledge. - 23:12

In matters of worship, this verse suggests that true reverence involves a willingness to receive discipline and correction. It prompts us to approach the teachings of wisdom with an open heart, recognizing that correction is a pathway to growth and spiritual maturity.

In summary, Proverbs 22 and 23 weave a tapestry of wisdom that illuminates worship and reverence. They call us to cultivate a good name, embrace humility and wisdom, teach righteousness, practice generosity, advocate for justice, and approach correction with an open heart. As we immerse ourselves in these verses, may our worship be deepened, our reverence heightened, and our lives become a testament to the timeless principles of wisdom illuminated by the Proverbs.

Meditation and Prayer Exercises

Embark on a transformative meditation and prayer journey, drawing inspiration from the profound wisdom of Proverbs 14-23. These exercises are designed to guide you in deepening your connection with the divine, cultivating mindfulness, and seeking the timeless insights woven into these chapters.

Meditation and Prayer Exercise 1: Seeking Divine Guidance
Verse Focus: Proverbs 20:24 - "The Lord directs our steps, so why try to understand everything along the way?"

Find a quiet space: Sit or lie down comfortably, creating an environment free from distractions.

Centering Breath: Take deep, intentional breaths. Inhale slowly, reflecting on the divine guidance that directs your steps. Exhale, releasing any uncertainties.

Reflective Meditation: Meditate on the concept of divine guidance. Picture your life journey as a path illuminated by the Lord. Allow a sense of trust and surrender to envelop you.

Prayer: Offer a prayer of surrender, acknowledging that your steps are directed by divine wisdom. Seek guidance for areas of your life where clarity is needed.

Meditation and Prayer Exercise 2: The Lamp of the Lord
Verse Focus: Proverbs 20:27 - "The Lord's light penetrates the human spirit, exposing every hidden motive."

Quiet Contemplation: Sit in a comfortable position. Close your eyes and focus on your breath. Allow your mind to settle.

Visual Imagery: Envision a gentle, radiant light within you, symbolizing the lamp of the Lord. Picture this light casting warmth and clarity on your innermost being.

Reflective Silence: Spend a few moments in silent reflection, allowing the divine light to reveal insights about your innermost self.

Expressive Prayer: Offer a prayer of gratitude for the divine light that illuminates your being. Seek guidance in aligning your spirit with the divine.

Meditation and Prayer Exercise 3: Cultivating Righteousness
Verse Focus: Proverbs 22:6 - "Direct your children onto the right path, and when they are older, they will not leave it."

Mindful Presence: Sit in a relaxed position. Bring your attention to the present moment, acknowledging the importance of righteous living.

Reflective Meditation: Contemplate the impact of teaching righteousness to the next generation. Visualize a chain of wisdom extending through time.

Prayer for Guidance: Offer a prayer for guidance in cultivating righteousness in your own life and those around you. Seek divine wisdom in your role as a guide.

Meditation and Prayer Exercise 4: A Banquet of Moderation

Verse Focus: Proverbs 23:1-3 - "While dining with a ruler, pay attention to what is put before you. If you are a big eater, put a knife to your throat; don't desire all the delicacies, for he might be trying to trick you."

Mindful Eating: If possible, prepare a simple meal. Sit down to eat with intentionality, savoring each bite.

Reflective Eating: Consider the wisdom of moderation as you eat. Reflect on the symbolism of a banquet and the choices you make in nourishing your body.

Gratitude Prayer: Offer a prayer of gratitude for the sustenance provided. Seek guidance in cultivating moderation and mindful eating as an act of reverence.

Meditation and Prayer Exercise 5: Humility and Wisdom

Verse Focus: Proverbs 22:4 (NIV) - "True humility and fear of the Lord lead to riches, honor, and long life."

The posture of Humility: Sit or kneel in a posture that symbolizes humility. Close your eyes and breathe deeply.

Contemplative Silence: Enter a moment of contemplative silence, acknowledging the divine connection between humility and the fear of the Lord.

Prayer for Humility: Offer a prayer expressing your desire for a humble heart. Seek the wisdom, riches, honor, and life that flow from a spirit grounded in humility and reverence.

Note to Leader for Group Discussion: These meditation and prayer exercises are intended to be adapted to your personal preferences and spiritual practices. As you engage in these moments of reflection, may the wisdom of Proverbs 14-23 guide you on a transformative journey of faith, mindfulness, and divine connection.

Chapter 7: Navigating Challenges and Temptations

Welcome to Chapter 7 of our journey through the timeless wisdom of Proverbs. In this pivotal section, we delve into the practical and often complex aspects of navigating challenges and resisting temptations. Proverbs, with its succinct and profound insights, serves as a trusted compass, offering guidance on the winding paths of life.

Life, as we know, is a tapestry woven with threads of joy and sorrow, triumphs and trials. In the realm of challenges and temptations, Proverbs provides a lantern to illuminate our way, offering both cautionary tales and uplifting encouragement. As we traverse this chapter, we will uncover the wisdom that equips us to make sound decisions, resist the allure of temptations, and emerge resilient in the face of adversity.

The pages ahead are not a mere collection of maxims; they are a map guiding us through the intricate landscapes of human experience. Whether it be the siren call of destructive temptations or the formidable hurdles that life presents, Proverbs beckons us to draw from its well of timeless truths.

As we embark on this exploration, let us open our hearts to the wisdom that awaits, knowing that within the verses of Proverbs 23-25, we find not only insights to navigate challenges but also a source of strength to resist the allure of tempting paths. May this chapter be a source of illumination and empowerment as we navigate the complexities of life, guided by the wisdom that has transcended centuries.

Overcoming Challenges with Wisdom

Challenges are threads that weave through our journey, demanding resilience, discernment, and unwavering resolve. Proverbs 23, a wellspring of timeless wisdom, offers profound insights into overcoming challenges with the guiding light of sagacity. Let us explore the verses of Proverbs 23 and glean wisdom that empowers us to face life's trials with grace and fortitude.

If you are a big eater, put a knife to your throat. - 23:2

This vivid metaphor underscores the significance of self-control, especially in areas that may lead to detriment. Overcoming challenges requires discipline and a willingness to confront our tendencies toward excess. The verse encourages us to take drastic measures, metaphorically speaking, to exercise control over our desires.

Don't wear yourself out trying to get rich. Be wise enough to know when to quit. - 23:4

In the pursuit of success, this verse serves as a poignant reminder to discern the true priorities in life. It encourages us to seek wealth wisely, recognizing that relentless striving, divorced from wisdom, can lead to exhaustion and an unfulfilled existence.

Commit yourself to instruction; listen carefully to words of knowledge. - 23:12

Wisdom often comes through the counsel of others. This verse urges us to be open-hearted and attentive to instruction, emphasizing that the application of knowledge is the key to overcoming challenges. Seeking guidance and learning from the experiences of others can pave the way for sound decision-making.

My child, listen and be wise: Keep your heart on the right course. - 23:19

The path to overcoming challenges begins with a receptive heart. This verse implores us to listen, to seek wisdom, and to set our hearts on the right path. It emphasizes the proactive role we play in cultivating wisdom and choosing a course that leads to triumph over challenges.

Listen to your father, who gave you life, and don't despise your mother when she is old. - 23:22

In times of challenge, the wisdom of those who have gone before us can be invaluable. This verse highlights the importance of respecting and heeding the guidance of our elders. Their experiences can provide valuable insights and a compass to navigate challenges.

Don't gaze at the wine, seeing how red it is, how it sparkles in the cup, how smoothly it goes down. - 23:31

Challenges often come in the guise of tempting choices. This verse advises against the allure of excesses, cautioning us not to be entranced by fleeting pleasures that may lead to adversity. It underscores the importance of moderation and self-discipline in navigating the allure of destructive paths.

In summary, Proverbs 23 unveils a tapestry of wisdom that equips us to overcome life's challenges with discernment, moderation, self-control, and a willingness to learn. As we internalize these timeless insights, may we face challenges with a spirit fortified by wisdom, navigating the intricate terrain of life with resilience and grace.

Resisting Temptation

Temptation, with its alluring whispers and subtle snares, is a formidable adversary on the journey of life. In Proverbs 24, a treasury of enduring wisdom, we discover insights that empower us to stand resilient against the allure of temptation. Let us embark on a journey through Proverbs 24 to glean timeless counsel on fortifying our hearts and minds against the wiles of seduction.

A house is built by wisdom and becomes strong through good sense. Through knowledge its rooms are filled with all sorts of precious riches and valuables. - 24:3-4

The foundation of resistance against temptation lies in wisdom and understanding. This verse likens our lives to a house, suggesting that a firm and wise foundation is essential. By cultivating knowledge and understanding, we fortify ourselves against the storms of temptation.

So don't go to war without wise guidance; victory depends on having many advisers. - 24:6

Temptation is akin to a battlefield, and victory requires strategic thinking. Seeking counsel and guidance from wi mentors and friends is a powerful strategy. This verse encourages us to recognize the collective strength in advice, fostering a community that supports our journey of resisting temptation.

Rescue those who are unjustly sentenced to die; save them as they stagger to their death. Don't excuse yourself by saying, "Look, we didn't know." For God understands all hearts, and he sees you. He who guards your soul knows you knew. He will repay all people as their actions deserve. - 24:11-12

Resisting temptation extends beyond personal struggles. This powerful passage challenges us to stand against injustice and apathy. By actively engaging in compassion and justice, we fortify ourselves against the temptation to turn a blind eye to the needs of others.

My child, eat honey, for it is good, and the honeycomb is sweet to the taste. In the same way, wisdom is sweet to your soul. If you find it, you will have a bright future, and your hopes will not be cut short. - 24:13-14

This vivid metaphor likens wisdom to the sweetness of honey. Embracing wisdom becomes a source of delight and satisfaction, offering a counterbalance to the transient allure of temptation. The sweetness of wisdom provides a lasting satisfaction that surpasses the fleeting pleasures of temptation.

Here are some further sayings of the wise: It is wrong to show favoritism when passing judgment. A judge who says to the wicked, "You are innocent," will be cursed by many people and denounced by the nations. But it will go well for those who convict the guilty; rich blessings will be showered on them. - 24:23-25

Guarding against temptation involves upholding principles of justice and righteousness. This passage emphasizes the importance of impartiality and integrity. By maintaining a steadfast commitment to truth and justice, we fortify our hearts against the compromise that temptation may attempt to bring.

I walked by the field of a lazy person, the vineyard of one with no common sense. I saw that it was overgrown with nettles. It was covered with weeds, and its walls were broken down. Then, as I looked and thought about it, I learned this lesson: A little extra sleep, a little more slumber, a little folding of the hands to rest—then poverty will pounce on you like a bandit; scarcity will attack you like an armed robber. - 24:30-34

Temptation often capitalizes on idleness and complacency. This passage warns against the dangers of laziness and the vulnerability it brings. By staying diligent and purposeful, we build a defense against the temptations that can sneak into the void created by inactivity.

In conclusion, Proverbs 24 unfolds as a manual for resisting temptation—a guide that directs us to build a foundation of wisdom, seek strategic counsel, remain diligent, stand against injustice, savor the sweetness of wisdom, and guard our hearts with integrity. May these timeless insights embolden us to navigate the intricate landscape of temptation with discernment, fortitude, and an unwavering commitment to wisdom.

Coping with Adversity

Adversity is an inevitable companion on life's journey, a rugged terrain that tests the mettle of our spirits. Proverbs 25, a treasury of timeless wisdom, unfolds as a guidebook for navigating the challenges that adversity presents. Let's embark on a journey through Proverbs 25 to glean insights that empower us to cope with adversity with resilience, grace, and enduring wisdom.

When arguing with your neighbor, don't betray another person's secret. - 25:9

In the throes of adversity, conflicts may arise. This verse advises a principled approach, emphasizing the importance of integrity even in the face of disputes. Coping with adversity involves navigating conflicts with wisdom, and holding onto ethical principles even when the storm rages.

Timely advice is lovely, like golden apples in a silver basket. - 25:11

The timing of our actions holds significance in coping with adversity. This verse paints a vivid picture, likening a well-timed ruling to exquisite apples of gold in a setting of silver. It underscores the importance of discerning the opportune moment for our responses to life's adversities.

To one who listens, valid criticism is like a gold earring or other gold jewelry. - 25:12

In adversity, the discipline of listening becomes paramount. This verse illustrates the value of heeding wise counsel, comparing it to precious gold. Coping with challenges involves a humble receptivity to the insights of those with wisdom, recognizing that their guidance can be a priceless asset.

Patience can persuade a prince, and soft speech can break bones. - 25:15

Patience is a virtue that resonates in the face of adversity. This verse suggests that a calm and patient approach holds the power to influence and bring about positive change. In times of hardship, cultivating patience becomes a potent tool for navigating challenges with grace.

Good news from far away is like cold water to the thirsty. - 25:25

Kind and refreshing words have the power to rejuvenate a weary soul. In times of adversity, the encouragement and support we extend to one another act as a soothing balm. This verse prompts us to be bearers of good news, providing comfort to those navigating stormy seas.

A person without self-control is like a city with broken-down walls. - 25:28

Maintaining composure amid adversity requires self-control. This verse draws a vivid analogy, likening a lack of self-control to breached city walls. It underscores the importance of fortifying our inner defenses, recognizing that a composed spirit is essential for coping with life's challenges.

In summary, Proverbs 25 unfolds as a reservoir of wisdom, guiding coping with adversity. Through patience, self-control, integrity, refreshing words, disciplined listening, and an understanding of the right timing, we equip ourselves to face life's challenges with resilience and poise. As we internalize these timeless insights, may we navigate the adversities of life with a spirit fortified by enduring wisdom.

Case Studies and Discussion Questions

Case Study 1: The Dilemma of Financial Priorities Proverbs 23:4 - "Don't wear yourself out trying to get rich. Be wise enough to know when to quit."

Situation: Jenna, a hardworking professional, is at a crossroads. She's driven by a desire for financial success but finds herself exhausted and constantly pursuing more. The pressure to get rich is taking a toll on her well-being.

Discussion Questions:

How does Proverbs 23:4 guide Jenna's situation?

What principles from this verse can Jenna apply to find a balance between financial aspirations and personal well-being?

How might Jenna's perspective on wealth change if she embraces the wisdom of Proverbs 23:4?

Case Study 2: The Struggle Against Sloth Proverbs 24:30-34 - "I walked by the field of a lazy person, the vineyard of one with no common sense. I saw that it was overgrown with nettles. It was covered with weeds, and its walls were broken down. Then, as I looked and thought about it, I learned this lesson: A little extra sleep, a little more slumber, a little folding of the hands to rest—then poverty will pounce on you like a bandit; scarcity will attack you like an armed robber."

Situation: Mark is a talented artist with great potential, but he often procrastinates and avoids putting in the necessary effort to develop his skills. As a result, he's falling behind in his career.

Discussion Questions:

How does Proverbs 24:30-34 apply to Mark's situation?

What are the consequences of Mark's procrastination, considering the principles in this passage?

How can Mark implement the wisdom from Proverbs 24 to overcome his tendency toward sloth and work toward success?

Case Study 3: Coping with Injustice in the Workplace Proverbs 24:23-25 - "Here are some further sayings of the wise: It is wrong to show favoritism when passing judgment. A judge who says to the wicked, "You are innocent," will be cursed by many people and denounced by the nations. But it will go well for those who convict the guilty; rich blessings will be showered on them."

Situation: Sarah, an employee, witnesses an unfair judgment against a colleague in the workplace. The supervisor shows partiality, and Sarah grapples with whether to speak up against the injustice.

Discussion Questions:

How does Proverbs 24:23-25 guide Sarah in dealing with injustice?

What might be the consequences of remaining silent in the face of partiality?

How can Sarah apply the wisdom from this passage to address the situation without compromising her integrity?

Reflection Questions: Wisdom in Daily Living

Applying Patience (Proverbs 25:15):

Reflect on a recent situation where patience was challenging. How might embracing patience have altered the outcome?

Self-Control in Adversity (Proverbs 25:28):

Consider a time when maintaining self-control was difficult during adversity. What strategies could have helped you exhibit greater self-control?

Responding to Conflict with Wisdom (Proverbs 25:9):

Share an experience where navigating conflict requires wisdom. How did you approach the situation, and what did you learn from the experience?

The Impact of Encouraging Words (Proverbs 25:25):

Recall a moment when you received encouraging words during a challenging time. How did those words influence your perspective and resilience?

Listening to Wise Counsel (Proverbs 25:12):

Think of a decision you made based on wise counsel. How did the outcome compare to situations where you didn't seek advice?

The Timing of Actions (Proverbs 25:11):

Describe a scenario where the timing of your actions played a crucial role. How did considering the opportune moment affect the results?

Note to Leader for Group Discussion: These case studies and reflection questions are designed to stimulate thoughtful discussions and personal introspection, allowing individuals to apply the wisdom found in Proverbs 23-25 to their daily lives.

Chapter 8: A Life of Integrity and Character

As we open the pages of Chapter 8, we step into the profound realm of integrity and character—a timeless cornerstone of a meaningful and purposeful life. In Proverbs 26-28, we encounter a wealth of wisdom that illuminates the path toward ethical living, underscoring the significance of authenticity, honesty, and a steadfast commitment to virtuous principles.

This chapter is a compass for those navigating the complexities of daily choices and ethical dilemmas. It draws from the deep well of Proverbs to guide us in cultivating a life marked by integrity—a life where our character, actions, and principles align in harmonious unity.

In a world often fraught with moral ambiguities, Proverbs 26-28 emerges as a beacon, offering insights that transcend cultural and temporal boundaries. Here, we find wisdom that not only shapes our character but also contributes to the fabric of a just and compassionate society.

As we embark on this exploration, let us delve into the verses with open hearts and receptive minds, ready to absorb the timeless truths that beckon us toward a life of integrity. May this chapter inspire us to weave the threads of virtue into the very fabric of our being, fostering a legacy that resonates with the enduring principles illuminated by the wisdom of Proverbs.

Developing Integrity and Character

In the tapestry of personal development, integrity and character form the intricate patterns that define our essence. Proverbs 26, a treasury of timeless wisdom, offers profound insights into the art of cultivating a life marked by authenticity and moral strength. Let's explore the verses of Proverbs 26 to glean lessons that guide us in the journey of developing integrity and character.

Don't answer the foolish arguments of fools, or you will become as foolish as they are. Be sure to answer the foolish arguments of fools, or they will become wise in their own estimation. - 26:4-5

Character is revealed in how we respond to others. This paradoxical wisdom calls for discernment in dealing with fools. Developing integrity involves choosing responses that reflect wisdom and self-control.

As a dog returns to its vomit, so a fool repeats his foolishness. - 26:11

Developing character involves recognizing and learning from past mistakes. This verse urges us to break the cycle of foolish behavior by embracing self-awareness and a commitment to growth.

As a door swings back and forth on its hinges, so the lazy person turns over in bed. - 26:14

Laziness erodes character. This verse emphasizes the importance of diligence and a proactive approach to life. Developing integrity requires a commitment to industry and purposeful action.

Lazy people consider themselves smarter than seven wise counselors. - 26:16

True character is demonstrated through consistent actions. This verse contrasts the self-perception of the lazy with the discreet actions of others. Developing integrity requires a humble recognition of our strengths and weaknesses.

Rumors are dainty morsels that sink deep into one's heart. - 26:22

Character is influenced by the company we keep. This verse underscores the impact of gossip on the integrity of relationships. Developing character involves choosing friends and associates who uphold ethical standards.

People may cover their hatred with pleasant words, but they're deceiving you. They pretend to be kind, but don't believe them. Their hearts are full of many evils. While their hatred may be concealed by trickery, their wrongdoing will be exposed in public. - 26:24-26

Deception erodes character from within. This passage warns against those who mask deceit with charm. Developing integrity involves discernment and a commitment to authentic communication.

A lying tongue hates its victims, and flattering words cause ruin. - 26:28

Dishonesty corrodes character. This verse illuminates the destructive nature of deceit. Developing integrity necessitates a commitment to truthfulness, even when faced with difficult circumstances.

In summary, Proverbs 26 unfolds as a guidebook for developing integrity and character—a journey marked by self-awareness, diligence, honesty, wise associations, discerning responses, consistency, and a rejection of deception. As we internalize these lessons, may we forge a character that stands resilient in the face of life's challenges, reflecting the enduring wisdom of Proverbs?

Living a Moral and Ethical Life

In the quest for a meaningful and purposeful existence, Proverbs 27 emerges as a guiding light, offering profound insights into the art of living a moral and ethical life. This chapter serves as a compass, navigating the complexities of human relationships, personal conduct, and the pursuit of virtue. Let's explore the verses of Proverbs 27 to glean wisdom that illuminates the path toward a life marked by moral integrity and ethical principles.

Don't brag about tomorrow, since you don't know what the day will bring. - 27:1

Moral living requires humility and an acknowledgment of life's uncertainties. This verse urges us to approach each day with a sense of humility, recognizing that ethical choices are made in the present, not in a future we may not witness.

Anger is cruel, and wrath is like a flood, but jealousy is even more dangerous. - 27:4

Moral living requires guarding against destructive emotions. This verse highlights the corrosive nature of jealousy. To live ethically is to cultivate contentment, celebrate the successes of others, and guard against the pitfalls of envy.

Wounds from a sincere friend are better than many kisses from an enemy. - 27:6

Living ethically involves embracing constructive criticism. This verse underscores the value of true friendship, where honest feedback, even if it stings, is a trustworthy guide. Constructive criticism is an essential component of personal growth and ethical living.

A person who is full refuses honey, but even bitter food tastes sweet to the hungry. - 27:7

Living ethically includes cultivating contentment. This verse prompts reflection on the impact of abundance on our perception. True ethical living involves appreciating and sharing one's blessings with those in need.

As iron sharpens iron, so a friend sharpens a friend. - 27:17

Ethical living flourishes in the context of accountable relationships. This verse paints a vivid image of mutual influence. It emphasizes the role of friends in refining each other's character, fostering growth, and promoting ethical conduct.

As a face is reflected in water, so the heart reflects the real person. - 27:19

Ethical living involves an understanding of our internal disposition. This verse likens life to a reflection in water, emphasizing that our actions mirror the condition of our hearts. To live ethically is to cultivate a heart attuned to moral principles.

Fire tests the purity of silver and gold, but a person is tested by being praised. - 27:21

Living ethically entails responding to praise with gratitude and responsibility. This verse compares people to precious metals refined by fire, highlighting the testing nature of praise. True ethical living involves humility in the face of recognition and a commitment to continue virtuous actions.

In summary, Proverbs 27 serves as a guidebook for those aspiring to live a moral and ethical life. Through lessons on constructive criticism, contentment, accountability, humility, heart condition, gratitude, and guarding against destructive emotions, this chapter illuminates the principles that underpin a life of virtue and ethical conduct. May these timeless insights inspire us to weave the fabric of our lives with threads of moral integrity and ethical excellence.

The Role of Wisdom in Community

Proverbs 28 stands as a testament to the profound impact of wisdom on the fabric of community life. Within its verses, we discover a wealth of insights that illuminate the role of wisdom in fostering harmony, justice, and prosperity within the collective. Let's delve into the verses of Proverbs 28 to unravel the principles that underscore the indispensable role of wisdom in nurturing a thriving and virtuous community.

When there is moral rot within a nation, its government topples easily. But wise and knowledgeable leaders bring stability. - 28:2

Wise leadership is the cornerstone of a flourishing community. This verse underscores the transformative power of discernment and knowledge in maintaining order and fostering stability within a collective.

Income from charging high interest rates will end up in the pocket of someone who is kind to the poor. - 28:8

Wisdom condemns the exploitation of the vulnerable. This verse illuminates the cyclical nature of injustice, emphasizing that ill-gotten wealth ultimately benefits those who act with kindness and compassion toward the less fortunate.

People who conceal their sins will not prosper, but if they confess and turn from them, they will receive mercy. - 28:13

Wisdom fosters a culture of accountability and forgiveness. This verse emphasizes the healing potential of confession within a community, creating an environment where individuals can openly address mistakes and seek collective mercy.

A ruler with no understanding will oppress his people, but one who hates corruption will have a long life. - 28:16

Wisdom abhors injustice. This verse highlights the precarious nature of leadership that thrives on extortion and contrasts it with the enduring stability of a ruler who upholds fairness and integrity.

In the end, people appreciate honest criticism far more than flattery. - 28:23

Wisdom values honest communication. This verse promotes the idea that a community built on sincere feedback and constructive criticism, rather than flattery, establishes a foundation of trust and mutual respect.

Greed causes fighting; trusting the Lord leads to prosperity. - 28:25

Wisdom encourages a spirit of trust and generosity. This verse contrasts the divisive impact of greed with the prosperity that arises from a community built on trust in a higher purpose.

Whoever gives to the poor will lack nothing, but those who close their eyes to poverty will be cursed. - 28:27

Wisdom fosters a spirit of generosity and compassion. This verse underscores the reciprocal nature of giving to the poor, suggesting that a community that embraces social responsibility reaps blessings in abundance.

In summary, Proverbs 28 unveils the pivotal role of wisdom in shaping a resilient and harmonious community. Through lessons on leadership, the impact of greed, the healing power of confession, fairness, social responsibility, the consequences of injustice, and the foundation of social trust, this chapter provides a blueprint for communities aspiring to thrive with virtue and wisdom. May these timeless insights inspire us to collectively cultivate wisdom and foster communities that reflect the enduring principles illuminated by the wisdom of Proverbs.

Character-Building Activities

1. Journal Reflection on Past Mistakes (Proverbs 26:11):
Activity: Encourage individuals to reflect on past mistakes and consider the lessons learned. Provide journals for self-reflection. Discuss the importance of recognizing folly to foster personal growth and character development.

2. Constructive Criticism Workshop (Proverbs 27:6):
Activity: Organize a workshop on giving and receiving constructive criticism. Create scenarios for practice and discussions. Emphasize the role of honest feedback in personal and professional growth.

3. Contentment Challenge (Proverbs 27:7):
Activity: Initiate a contentment challenge where participants focus on appreciating what they have. Encourage them to share experiences of finding joy in simplicity. Discuss how contentment contributes to a morally centered life.

4. Accountability Partnerships (Proverbs 27:17):
Activity: Pair individuals as accountability partners. Have regular check-ins where they discuss personal goals, challenges, and progress. Emphasize the role of supportive friendships in character development.

5. Wisdom in Leadership Seminar (Proverbs 28:2):
Activity: Host a leadership seminar exploring the principles of discernment and knowledge in maintaining order. Invite wise leaders to share their experiences. Discuss how ethical leadership contributes to community well-being.

6. Acts of Generosity Campaign (Proverbs 28:25):
Activity: Launch a community campaign to promote acts of generosity. Encourage participants to perform random acts of kindness and share their experiences. Discuss the impact of generosity on community cohesion.

7. Confession and Forgiveness Circle (Proverbs 28:13):
Activity: Create a safe space for confession and forgiveness. Facilitate a circle where participants share their experiences of confessing mistakes and seeking forgiveness. Discuss the healing power of sincere confession.

8. Fair Trade Fair (Proverbs 28:16):
Activity: Organize a fair trade fair featuring products that adhere to ethical and fair-trade principles. Discuss the impact of supporting fair practices on global and local communities.

9. Community Service Day (Proverbs 28:27):
Activity: Plan a community service day where participants volunteer for various causes. Reflect on the experience and discuss the reciprocal nature of giving to the less fortunate.

10. Ethical Decision-Making Workshop (Proverbs 28:8): - Activity: Conduct a workshop on ethical decision-making. Present case studies and engage participants in discussions about the consequences of unjust practices. Emphasize the importance of making morally sound choices.

11. Honesty in Communication Exercise (Proverbs 28:23): - **Activity:** Facilitate an exercise on honest communication. Provide scenarios for participants to practice delivering constructive feedback with sincerity. Discuss the importance of trust in building a strong community.

Note to Leader for Group Discussion: These character-building activities are designed to engage individuals and communities in practical experiences inspired by the wisdom found in Proverbs 26-28. Each activity focuses on key principles such as self-reflection, constructive criticism, contentment, accountability, wisdom in leadership, generosity, confession, fairness, community service, ethical decision-making, and honest communication. Through these activities, participants can internalize and apply the timeless wisdom embedded in these Proverbs to shape their character and contribute to the betterment of their communities.

Chapter 9: Community and Servant Leadership

Embark on a journey through Proverbs 29-31 as we explore timeless principles of community dynamics and servant leadership. In Proverbs 29, we delve into the impact of righteous leadership on communal well-being and the significance of empathy and social justice in servant leadership. The chapter also underscores the pivotal role of wisdom in maintaining societal order.

Transitioning to Proverbs 31, we celebrate the value of virtuous character, especially in women, recognizing their contributions to community strength. The chapter concludes with a vivid illustration of servant leadership in daily acts, prompting reflection on how such practices can inspire leaders within our communities.

Throughout this exploration, we aim to unravel insights that guide us toward fostering communities characterized by righteousness, empathy, wisdom, and virtuous character. This journey invites us to reimagine leadership as a service-oriented endeavor, contributing to the harmonious tapestry of collective life.

Servant Leadership and Social Responsibility

In the pages of Proverbs 29, we unearth profound insights into the interplay of servant leadership and social responsibility, drawing from verses that illuminate the transformative influence of leaders who prioritize the well-being of their community and underscore our collective responsibility for societal welfare.

When the godly are in authority, the people rejoice. But when the wicked are in power, they groan. – 29:2

Proverbs 29 commences by illustrating the profound impact of righteous leadership on the collective spirit. The verse resonates with the idea that a community experiences joy and prosperity when guided by leaders of integrity.

The godly care about the rights of the poor; the wicked don't care at all. – 29:7

The chapter delves into the compassionate core of servant leadership, emphasizing the inherent care for justice for the poor. This verse draws a stark contrast, highlighting the indifferent stance of the wicked toward the marginalized.

The bloodthirsty hate blameless people, but the upright seek to help them. – 29:10

Implicit in Proverbs 29 is the concept that a righteous leader, embodying integrity and uprightness, may face challenges. The verse underscores the empathy-driven nature of servant leadership, where leaders stand firm for justice even in the face of opposition.

If a king judges the poor fairly, his throne will last forever. – 29:14

This verse subtly issues a call to social responsibility by emphasizing the importance of fair judgment, particularly for the poor. It underscores that societal well-being is intricately tied to leaders embracing their responsibility to ensure justice for all.

When people do not accept divine guidance, they run wild. But whoever obeys the law is joyful. – 29:18

Proverbs 29 underscores the pivotal role of wisdom in maintaining societal order. Leaders who heed wisdom's instruction contribute to stability and prosperity, aligning with the ethos of servant leadership that prioritizes the collective over the self.

Proverbs 29, with its wisdom-laden verses, beckons leaders to embody righteousness, cultivate empathy, and champion justice. This chapter serves as a timeless guide, urging communities to thrive through servant leadership and recognize the shared responsibility for social welfare. As we glean from these verses, may we be inspired to weave these principles into our leadership narratives, fostering a culture of servant leadership and social responsibility for the benefit of all.

Engaging in Acts of Kindness

In the reflective verses of Proverbs 30, a subtle yet profound invitation is extended—an invitation to engage in acts of kindness that resonate with the essence of wisdom. Proverbs 30 provides insights into the humility and virtuous living that underpin genuine acts of kindness, inviting us to embrace these principles in our interactions with others.

I am too stupid to be human, and I lack common sense. I have not mastered human wisdom, nor do I know the Holy One. – 30:2-3

The humility echoed in these verses lays the groundwork for acts of kindness. Acknowledging our limitations and being humble in our interactions with others opens the door to genuine compassion and understanding.

Every word of God proves true. He is a shield to all who come to him for protection. – 30:5

Acts of kindness are rooted in a belief in goodness, and Proverbs 30 reminds us that seeking refuge in the virtuous path outlined by God's words provides a shield of protection. Acts of kindness, therefore, become a manifestation of this refuge.

First, help me never to tell a lie. Second, give me neither poverty nor riches! Give me just enough to satisfy my needs. For if I grow rich, I may deny you and say, "Who is the Lord?" And if I am too poor, I may steal and thus insult God's holy name. – 30:8-9

Contentment is a cornerstone for acts of kindness. These verses prompt reflection on the balance between our needs and wants, fostering an appreciation for sufficiency and, in turn, a willingness to share with others.

There are three things that make the earth tremble—no, four it cannot endure: a slave who becomes a king, an overbearing fool who prospers, a bitter woman who finally gets a husband, a servant girl who supplants her mistress. – 30:21-23

The verses highlight the impact of societal disruptions, emphasizing the importance of treating others with respect and fairness. Acts of kindness are woven into the fabric of respecting the dignity of every individual, regardless of their station in life.

If you have been a fool by being proud or plotting evil, cover your mouth in shame. – 30:32

These words serve as a gentle reminder to nurture gratitude in our hearts. Acts of kindness emanate from a spirit of humility and gratitude, discouraging self-centered actions that may harm others.

In essence, Proverbs 30 extends an invitation to engage in acts of kindness that are deeply rooted in humility, goodness, contentment, respect, and gratitude. As we absorb the wisdom within these verses, may our actions reflect the gentle yet transformative power of kindness, enriching the lives of those around us and fostering a community where compassion is the cornerstone of virtuous living.

Role Models and Inspiring Stories

Within the timeless wisdom of Proverbs 31, we encounter a rich tapestry of virtues that depict an exemplary woman—a role model whose life serves as an inspiration and source of guidance. The verses of Proverbs 31 offer not only a portrait of noble character but also unfold inspiring stories of strength, wisdom, and compassion, inviting us to reflect on the qualities that make a person worthy of emulation.

Who can find a virtuous and capable wife? She is more precious than rubies. Her husband can trust her, and she will greatly enrich his life. She brings him good, not harm, all the days of her life. – 31:10-12

These verses paint a portrait of a woman of noble character, emphasizing her immense value. Her role as a supportive and trustworthy partner sets the stage for inspiring stories of commitment and mutual respect.

She finds wool and flax and busily spins it. She is like a merchant's ship, bringing her food from afar. She gets up before dawn to prepare breakfast for her household and plan the day's work for her servant girls. She goes to inspect a field and buys it; with her earnings she plants a vineyard. – 31:13-16

These verses unfold an inspiring story of industriousness and an entrepreneurial spirit. The woman described in Proverbs 31 is not only diligent but also resourceful, embodying qualities that resonate with those who aspire to turn their talents into meaningful contributions.

She extends a helping hand to the poor and opens her arms to the needy. – 31:20

An inspiring story unfolds as the virtuous woman extends her compassion beyond her immediate circle, reaching out to the poor and needy. Her actions exemplify the transformative power of kindness and generosity.

When she speaks, her words are wise, and she gives instructions with kindness. – 31:26

The woman of noble character is characterized by wisdom and grace in her speech. Her inspiring story revolves around the influence of words that uplift and instruct, emphasizing the impact of mindful communication.

Her children stand and bless her. Her husband praises her: "There are many virtuous and capable women in the world, but you surpass them all!" – 31:28-29

The closing verses unveil an inspiring story of a woman whose legacy is one of honor and virtue. Her family recognizes and celebrates her contributions, highlighting the enduring impact of a life lived with purpose and integrity.

In Proverbs 31, we find not just a set of virtues but a collection of inspiring stories that resonate across generations. The woman depicted serves as a role model, embodying qualities of character, industriousness, compassion, wisdom, and legacy. As we explore these verses, may we draw inspiration from the timeless wisdom they offer, allowing the stories within Proverbs 31 to guide our journeys toward becoming role models and sources of inspiration in the lives of those around us.

Group Service Projects

Engaging in service projects as a group provides a tangible way to embody the virtues outlined in Proverbs 29-31. These projects can serve as expressions of righteousness, compassion, wisdom, and humility, fostering a sense of communal well-being. Here are some group service project ideas inspired by the wisdom of Proverbs:

Community Clean-Up and Restoration: Project Inspiration: Proverbs 31:8-9 encourages advocacy for justice and the rights of the oppressed. Organize a group clean-up and restoration project in a disadvantaged community, addressing both environmental concerns and supporting those in need.

Women's Empowerment Workshop: Project Inspiration: Proverbs 31 celebrates the virtues of a capable and empowered woman. Conduct workshops focused on empowering women with practical skills, career guidance, and self-esteem building.

Food Drive and Distribution: Project Inspiration: Reflecting Proverbs 29:7, organize a food drive to support local food banks or shelters. Distribute collected items to those in need, emphasizing care for the less fortunate.

Wisdom Sharing Sessions: Project Inspiration: Following Proverbs 29:18, host wisdom-sharing sessions within your community. Invite speakers to share insights on various topics, fostering an atmosphere of learning and collective wisdom.

Home Renovation for the Needy: Project Inspiration: Proverbs 31:20 highlights compassion for the poor. Collaborate on a home renovation project to improve living conditions for families facing financial hardship.

Mentoring and Tutoring Program: Project Inspiration: Inspired by Proverbs 29:15, initiate a group mentoring and tutoring program for children in underserved communities. Provide academic support and mentorship to help them thrive.

Community Garden Project: Project Inspiration: Proverbs 31:16 encourages industriousness. Establish a community garden to promote sustainable living, provide fresh produce for those in need, and teach valuable agricultural skills.

Care Packages for the Elderly: Project Inspiration: Reflecting Proverbs 31:28, create care packages for elderly individuals in assisted living facilities. Include essential items, letters of encouragement, and handmade crafts to bring joy to their lives.

Workshops on Financial Literacy: Project Inspiration: Proverbs 31:16-18 emphasizes prudent financial management. Conduct workshops on financial literacy to empower individuals and families with budgeting and savings skills.

Support for Single Parents: Project Inspiration: Proverbs 31:8-9 advocates for those in need. Extend support to single parents by organizing events, offering childcare services, or creating a support network to ease the challenges they face.

Clothing Drive and Distribution: Project Inspiration: Proverbs 31:21 encourages providing warm clothing. Organize a clothing drive and distribute collected items to homeless shelters or communities facing economic hardship.

12. Environmental Stewardship Project: Project Inspiration: Reflecting the wisdom of Proverbs, organize an environmental stewardship project such as tree planting, recycling initiatives, or campaigns to raise awareness about sustainable practices.

Note to Leader for Group Discussion: Engaging in these group service projects not only reflects the virtues and wisdom found in Proverbs 29-31 but also provides an opportunity for meaningful impact in your community. As a collective, your actions can embody the principles of righteousness, compassion, wisdom, and humility, creating a positive ripple effect in the lives of those you serve.

Conclusion

As we conclude our exploration through the rich tapestry of the Book of Proverbs, we find ourselves woven into the timeless fabric of wisdom, compassion, and virtue. Proverbs, a collection of profound insights and practical guidance, has been our compass through the complexities of life in the 21st century.

From the opening chapters that beckon us to embrace wisdom's call, to the poignant narratives of Proverbs 29-31 that illuminate the virtues of righteousness, compassion, and industriousness, we have traversed a journey of self-discovery and communal betterment.

The call to embody the wisdom of Proverbs is not a distant echo from the past; rather, it reverberates through the challenges and opportunities of our contemporary world. Proverbs beckon us to be righteous leaders, compassionate neighbors, and individuals of virtuous character in a landscape often marked by tumult.

In applying the wisdom of Proverbs to our lives, we've explored practical ways to navigate relationships, make wise decisions, and foster personal and communal growth. We've considered the relevance of Proverbs in addressing contemporary issues and guiding us through the intricacies of work, wealth, and the pursuit of a balanced life.

As we reflect on the wisdom encapsulated in this ancient text, let us carry forward the lessons learned into our daily lives. Let our decisions be shaped by discernment, our relationships be nurtured with kindness, and our leadership be marked by humility and justice.

Proverbs extend an enduring invitation to a life of purpose, guided by principles that transcend time and culture. It calls us to be architects of positive change in our communities, embracing the responsibility to uplift the downtrodden and champion justice for the marginalized.

In our collective journey through this exploration of Proverbs, may we continue to seek wisdom, cultivate compassion, and live with integrity. Let us be inspired by the ageless truths contained within these verses, recognizing that, in applying the wisdom of Proverbs, we contribute to a more harmonious and virtuous world.

As we close this chapter, let the wisdom of Proverbs linger in our hearts, shaping our thoughts, actions, and aspirations. For in the pages of Proverbs, we discover not just a collection of ancient sayings, but a timeless guide for a life well-lived—a tapestry of wisdom that spans the ages and resonates with the aspirations of the 21st-century seeker of truth.

Recap of Key Takeaways

Wisdom as a Guiding Light:

Proverbs opens with an invitation to embrace wisdom as a guiding light in our lives. The pursuit of wisdom is a continual journey, one that shapes our decisions, relationships, and character.

Leadership Rooted in Righteousness:

Proverbs 29 emphasizes the profound impact of righteous leadership on community well-being. A righteous leader fosters joy and prosperity, and Proverbs calls us to embody such leadership in our spheres of influence.

Compassion for the Vulnerable:

Proverbs 29-31 highlights the importance of compassion, especially for the poor and marginalized. Acts of kindness and social responsibility are woven into the fabric of a virtuous life, echoing the call to care for those in need.

Industriousness and Wisdom in Action:

The virtues celebrated in Proverbs 29-31 are not abstract ideals but principles to be lived. The industriousness of the capable woman, the wisdom in decision-making, and the entrepreneurial spirit are all actionable elements of a purposeful life.

Empowerment and Respect for Women:

Proverbs 31 provides a powerful portrayal of a virtuous woman, celebrating her strength, wisdom, and contributions. This stands as a call for the empowerment and respect of women in all aspects of life.

Balancing Work, Wealth, and Life:

Proverbs offers practical wisdom on balancing the pursuit of success with a mindful and balanced life. It encourages ethical business practices, financial prudence, and a holistic approach to prosperity.

The Fear of the Lord:

Understanding the fear of the Lord, as outlined in Proverbs, involves reverence, humility, and a commitment to moral and ethical living. It forms the foundation for a life of wisdom and spiritual depth.

Navigating Challenges with Integrity:

Proverbs 23-25 provides insights into overcoming challenges with wisdom and maintaining integrity. It encourages resilience in the face of adversity and a steadfast commitment to ethical living.

Developing Integrity and Character:

Proverbs 26-28 emphasizes the importance of developing integrity and character. It highlights the role of wisdom in shaping individuals who contribute positively to their communities.

Community and Servant Leadership:

Proverbs 29-31 calls for community engagement, emphasizing servant leadership and social responsibility. Acts of kindness, mentorship programs, and support for the vulnerable become expressions of communal well-being.

Reflection on Virtuous Living:

Proverbs 31 invites reflection on the virtues that define a life well-lived. It encourages gratitude, humility, and a legacy of honor and virtue that transcends individual accomplishments.

Applying Ancient Wisdom in the Modern World:

The wisdom of Proverbs is not confined to the past; it is a living guide for navigating the complexities of the 21st century. Applying its principles fosters personal growth, communal harmony, and a commitment to justice and compassion.

Personal Transformations

Proverbs has been more than a book; it's been a companion in my transformation. As I delved into the wisdom of Proverbs, I found that the ancient verses resonated with my contemporary experiences, triggering profound shifts in how I perceive and navigate life.

In the quiet moments of reflection, I discovered that embracing a wisdom-centric lifestyle wasn't just about making informed decisions; it was about infusing my choices with a deeper understanding of morality and ethics. It became a guiding light, illuminating a path where every decision was an opportunity to embody the wisdom I sought.

Leadership, once a distant concept, took on a new meaning. Proverbs 29's insights on righteous leadership challenged me to lead not for the sake of power but to foster joy and prosperity in the lives I touched. I realized that true leadership wasn't about authority but about creating a positive impact.

Compassion, a virtue often discussed but not always lived, became a daily practice. Acts of kindness weren't grand gestures but small, intentional efforts to connect with others. Proverbs 29-31 whispered to my soul, urging me to actively seek opportunities to make a difference in the lives of those around me, especially the vulnerable.

The practical wisdom embedded in Proverbs wasn't confined to ancient scrolls; it was a toolkit for navigating the complexities of my modern life. Industriousness, wise decision-making, and an entrepreneurial spirit weren't abstract ideals but actionable principles that transformed the way I approached my personal and professional endeavors.

The celebration of the capable woman in Proverbs 31 struck a chord deep within me. It fueled a commitment to championing the empowerment and respect of women in all aspects of life, reshaping my perspectives and actions.

Balancing work, wealth, and life ceased to be a theoretical exercise. Proverbs' guidance became a compass, leading me to reevaluate priorities and embrace a holistic approach to prosperity. Ethical business practices and financial prudence weren't just concepts but values woven into the fabric of my daily existence.

The fear of the Lord, a phrase that once seemed distant, became an intimate exploration of spirituality. It wasn't just about reverence; it was about cultivating a personal connection, and a moral compass that guided my choices and actions.

In moments of adversity, Proverbs 23-25 provides a comforting embrace. Navigating challenges with integrity wasn't just a lofty ideal; it was a resilient stance and a commitment to maintaining my ethical core even when faced with difficulties.

The focus on developing integrity and character wasn't a passive endeavor. It involved actively engaging in character-building activities, recognizing that personal growth was intricately tied to the virtues I embodied in my everyday interactions.

Community engagement, servant leadership, and social responsibility weren't abstract concepts but became the essence of my involvement in projects that contributed to communal well-being. The call to uplift the marginalized wasn't just a distant echo; it became a personal mission.

Reflections on virtuous living weren't detached philosophical musings. They prompted me to cultivate gratitude, humility, and a legacy of honor and virtue in the unique context of my life. Each day became an opportunity to reflect on the impact I wished to have on my family, my community, and the broader world.

Integration of ancient wisdom into my modern life wasn't a theoretical exercise. It manifested in tangible shifts, guiding my decisions, shaping my relationships, and fostering a harmonious and compassionate existence. "Wisdom Unveiled" wasn't just a book; it was a catalyst for my evolution, a companion in the intimate exploration of what it means to live a life enriched by timeless wisdom.

Encouragement to Continue the Journey

As we conclude our transformative journey through the profound teachings of Proverbs, let this not be the end but rather a significant waypoint in the ongoing adventure of wisdom and self-discovery. Completing this study is not the culmination but the commencement of a life continually enriched by the timeless truths we've encountered.

In the pages of Proverbs, we've uncovered a treasury of wisdom that speaks to the very fabric of our existence. It has been more than a study; it has been a journey into the depths of our souls, challenging us to reflect on our beliefs, actions, and the very essence of our character.

As we stand at this juncture, let us not view it as a conclusion but as a launching pad for a life imbued with the wisdom we've gleaned. The wisdom of Proverbs is not meant to be confined to a study session; it's designed to be lived, breathed, and woven into the tapestry of our everyday existence.

If you have found this Study useful in your life, please share it with other. Please consider leaving an honest revies online.

God Bless.

Here's an encouragement to continue the journey:

1. Embrace Daily Reflection:
Take a few moments each day for quiet reflection. Consider the wisdom of Proverbs in the context of your daily experiences. How can its teachings shape your interactions, decisions, and responses?

2. Engage in Continuous Learning:
Wisdom is a lifelong pursuit. Explore other spiritual texts, philosophical teachings, or writings that align with the principles you've discovered in Proverbs. Every piece of wisdom encountered adds depth to your understanding.

3. Apply Wisdom in Action:
Wisdom is not theoretical; it's practical. Actively seek opportunities to apply the insights gained. Whether it's in your relationships, work, or community involvement, let the wisdom of Proverbs guide your actions.

4. Share the Journey:
Wisdom deepens when shared. Engage in conversations with fellow seekers or start a study group. Share your reflections, learn from others, and collectively enrich your understanding of the timeless truths we've explored.

5. Cultivate a Heart of Gratitude:
Gratitude is a powerful expression of wisdom. Cultivate a daily practice of gratitude. Reflect on the blessings in your life and express thanks. Gratitude opens the heart to the transformative power of wisdom.

6. Embrace Challenges with Wisdom:
Life is a series of challenges and triumphs. As you encounter difficulties, approach them with the resilience and wisdom you've cultivated. Proverbs provide a sturdy foundation for navigating the complexities of life.

7. Foster a Spirit of Humility:
The journey of wisdom is marked by humility. Recognize that wisdom is a lifelong pursuit, and there is always more to learn. Approach each day with a humble heart, open to the lessons it brings.

8. Establish Rituals of Connection:
Create rituals that connect you to the wisdom you've gained. Whether it's a daily prayer, meditation, or moments of silence, establish practices that keep you grounded in the principles that have touched your soul.

9. Seek Guidance in Times of Decision:
When faced with significant decisions, turn to the wisdom of Proverbs for guidance. Let its teachings be a compass, helping you navigate the complexities and make choices aligned with your values.

10. Celebrate Your Growth:
Acknowledge and celebrate the growth you've experienced. Transformation is a journey, not a destination. Celebrate the small victories, and appreciate the person you are becoming through the pursuit of wisdom.

May this not be a farewell but a commencement into a life enriched by the wisdom of Proverbs. The journey continues, and with each step, may you find deeper meaning, purpose, and fulfillment.

Workbook Pages and Study Material

Chapter 1: Introduction to Proverbs and the Call of Wisdom

Opening Reflection:
What motivated you to embark on a study of the Book of Proverbs? Share your expectations and personal goals for this journey.

Exploring the Nature of Wisdom:
How does Proverbs define wisdom, and what attributes are associated with a wise person? Consider personal examples of wisdom in action.

Contextual Understanding:
Reflect on the historical and cultural context of Proverbs. How might the cultural background influence the interpretation of certain proverbs?

Key Themes and Purposes:
Identify the key themes introduced in Proverbs 1. How do these themes align with the overall purposes of the book?

Application to the 21st Century:
Consider the relevance of Proverbs to contemporary issues. How can the wisdom presented in this ancient text be applied to challenges and situations in our 21st-century world?

Interpreting Proverbs:
Proverbs often use symbolic language and metaphors. Choose a specific proverb from Chapter 1 and discuss different interpretations or applications.

Critical Thinking:
How does the introductory chapter set the tone for the entire Book of Proverbs? Explore the connections between the introduction and the subsequent chapters.

Personal Reflection:
Share a proverb or piece of wisdom that has been particularly impactful for you. Why does it resonate with you, and how have you applied it in your life?

Future Study Considerations:
As you conclude Chapter 1, what aspects or questions would you like to explore further in the subsequent chapters of the Book of Proverbs?

Group Discussion:
Engage in a group discussion about the diverse perspectives within the group regarding the concept of wisdom. How do cultural backgrounds or individual experiences shape these perspectives?

Chapter 2: Applying Proverbs in the Modern World

Personal Reflection:

How has your understanding of wisdom evolved after delving into the Book of Proverbs, and how do you envision applying this wisdom in your daily life?

Wisdom in Everyday Life:

Using Proverbs 1 as an example, explore how the text encourages the application of wisdom in everyday situations. Share instances where you've seen wisdom at work in mundane activities.

Decision-Making and Proverbs:

Discuss Proverbs 1:7, "The fear of the Lord is the beginning of knowledge." How does this principle inform decision-making in your life? Share an experience where reverence for God played a role in your choices.

Practical Application:

Choose a specific proverb from Proverbs 1 and discuss practical ways to apply its wisdom in contemporary scenarios. How does it relate to challenges faced in the 21st century?

Interconnected Themes:

Explore the interconnected themes introduced in Proverbs 1 and 2. How do concepts such as wisdom, understanding, and knowledge relate to one another in the pursuit of a meaningful life?

Relevance to Contemporary Issues:

Consider a current societal issue or challenge. How might the wisdom presented in Proverbs 1 and 2 provide insights or guidance in addressing this issue?

Cultural Sensitivity:

Discuss the importance of cultural sensitivity when applying the principles of Proverbs in a diverse and globalized world. How can wisdom be universally relevant while respecting cultural differences?

Critical Thinking:

Critically analyze the notion of "the fear of the Lord" in Proverbs 1 and 2. How does it contribute to the overall message of the text, and how can it be understood in a contemporary context?

Personal Application Challenges:

Identify a specific challenge or area of your life where applying the wisdom of Proverbs might be particularly challenging. Discuss strategies for overcoming these challenges.

Group Discussion:

Engage in a group discussion about the various perspectives on the practical application of Proverbs in the modern world. How do different individuals interpret and apply the wisdom in their unique contexts?

Chapter 3: The Pursuit of Wisdom (Proverbs 4, 5, and 6)

Reflecting on Wisdom:

How is wisdom portrayed in Proverbs 4, 5, and 6? Share your insights into the nature of wisdom as presented in these chapters.

Nature of Wisdom (Proverbs 4):

Explore the metaphor of the "path of the righteous" in Proverbs 4. How does this image contribute to our understanding of the nature of wisdom?

Seeking Wisdom (Proverbs 5):

Proverbs 5 warns against the pitfalls of straying from the path of wisdom. Discuss the importance of actively seeking wisdom and the consequences of neglecting it.

Consequences of Folly (Proverbs 6):

Proverbs 6 provides a list of actions considered foolish. How do these examples illustrate the consequences of failing to embrace wisdom?

Balancing Individual Freedom and Wisdom:

Reflect on the tension between individual freedom and the guidance of wisdom in these chapters. How can one strike a balance between personal autonomy and the pursuit of wisdom?

Wisdom in Decision-Making:

Share a personal experience where the pursuit of wisdom played a crucial role in decision-making. What was the outcome, and what did you learn from the experience?

Relating to Others (Proverbs 5):

Proverbs 5 addresses the importance of faithfulness in relationships. Discuss the relevance of these principles in contemporary contexts, including friendships and romantic relationships.

Wisdom and Character Development:

How do the teachings in Proverbs 4, 5, and 6 contribute to the development of one's character? Discuss the role of wisdom in shaping personal integrity.

Critical Thinking:

Analyze the metaphor of the "adulteress" in Proverbs 5. What broader principles or warnings might this metaphor convey about temptation and unwise choices?

Application Challenges:

Identify specific challenges in your life where the pursuit of wisdom, as outlined in Proverbs 4, 5, and 6, might be challenging. How can you overcome these challenges?

Group Reflection:

Engage in a group discussion about the collective insights gained from Proverbs 4, 5, and 6. How can the pursuit of wisdom contribute to the well-being of the community?

Chapter 4: Relationships and Communication (Proverbs 6 to 9)

Reflecting on Relationship Wisdom:

How does Proverbs 6 to 9 contribute to our understanding of relationships and communication? Share your reflections on the insights presented in these chapters.

Introduction to Chapter 4:

How does the opening of Proverbs 6 set the stage for discussions on relationships and communication? Explore the initial verses and their relevance to interpersonal dynamics.

Wisdom in Friendships (Proverbs 6):

Proverbs 6 warns against becoming surety for a friend. Discuss the implications of this advice on trust, friendship, and personal responsibility in relationships.

Adulterous Woman and Folly (Proverbs 6 and 7):

Analyze the metaphorical use of the adulterous woman in Proverbs 6 and 7. What broader insights does it provide about the dangers of temptation and unwise associations?

Invitations of Wisdom (Proverbs 8):

Explore the personification of Wisdom in Proverbs 8. What characteristics and attributes are associated with Wisdom, and how might these qualities enhance relationships?

Contrasting Paths (Proverbs 8 and 9):

Compare and contrast the paths of Wisdom and Folly as presented in Proverbs 8 and 9. How do these paths influence one's approach to relationships and communication?

Wisdom's Call (Proverbs 8):

Reflect on the universal call of Wisdom in Proverbs 8. How might embracing wisdom transform the way we communicate and relate to others in diverse contexts?

Communication and Understanding (Proverbs 9):

Proverbs 9 emphasizes the importance of understanding in communication. Discuss the role of understanding in fostering healthy relationships and resolving conflicts.

Applying Relationship Wisdom:

Share a personal experience where the wisdom of Proverbs influenced your approach to a relationship or communication challenge. What lessons did you draw from that experience?

Navigating Difficult Relationships (Proverbs 6-9):

Consider the practical advice given in Proverbs 6 to 9. How might this wisdom be applied to navigate challenges in difficult or strained relationships?

Critical Thinking:

Analyze the cultural and historical context of Proverbs 6 to 9. How might the societal norms of the time influence the guidance provided on relationships and communication?

Group Discussion:

Engage in a group discussion about the collective wisdom gained from Proverbs 6 to 9. How can the principles discussed contribute to building healthier and more meaningful relationships within the community?

Chapter 5: Work, Wealth, and Success (Proverbs 10 to 13)

Reflecting on Principles of Success:

How do Proverbs 10 to 13 contribute to our understanding of work, wealth, and success? Share your insights and reflections on the principles presented in these chapters.

Introduction to Chapter 5:

Explore the opening verses of Proverbs 10 and 11. How do these verses set the tone for discussions on work, wealth, and success in these chapters?

Prosperity and Diligence (Proverbs 10 and 11):

Discuss the relationship between prosperity and diligence as portrayed in Proverbs 10 and 11. How does the text encourage a balanced perspective on wealth and hard work?

Ethical Business Practices (Proverbs 12):

Proverbs 12 addresses the importance of ethical business practices. How can these principles guide individuals in the workplace, and what impact might they have on broader societal ethics?

Balancing Work and Life (Proverbs 13):

Reflect on the guidance provided in Proverbs 13 regarding the balance between work and life. How might this wisdom influence one's approach to time management and priorities?

Wealth and Generosity (Proverbs 11 and 12):

Discuss the concept of wealth and generosity in Proverbs 11 and 12. How do these principles challenge common perceptions of success, especially in a materialistic society?

Practical Wisdom for Success (Proverbs 10 to 13):

Identify specific pieces of practical wisdom for success found in Proverbs 10 to 13. How can these nuggets of wisdom be applied in contemporary professional and personal settings?

The Tongue and Success (Proverbs 10 to 12):

Explore the recurring theme of the tongue and its impact on success in Proverbs 10 to 12. How can communication skills contribute to or hinder one's journey toward success?

Critical Thinking:

Analyze the cultural and historical context of Proverbs 10 to 13. How might the economic and social conditions of the time influence the guidance provided on work, wealth, and success?

Personal Application Challenges:

Identify specific challenges related to work, wealth, and success that you currently face. How might the principles in Proverbs 10 to 13 guide you in addressing these challenges?

Group Discussion:

Engage in a group discussion about the collective wisdom gained from Proverbs 10 to 13. How can the principles discussed contribute to a healthier and more balanced approach to work and success within the community?

Chapter 6: The Fear of the Lord and Faithful Living (Proverbs 14 to 17)

Reflecting on Faithful Living:

How do Proverbs 14 to 17 contribute to our understanding of faithful living and the fear of the Lord? Share your insights and reflections on the principles presented in these chapters.

Introduction to Chapter 6:

Explore the opening verses of Proverbs 14. How do these verses set the tone for discussions on faithful living and the fear of the Lord in these chapters?

Understanding the Fear of the Lord (Proverbs 14 and 15):

Discuss the concept of the fear of the Lord as presented in Proverbs 14 and 15. How does this fear influence one's attitudes, actions, and decision-making?

Implications for Faith and Spirituality (Proverbs 16):

Reflect on the implications for faith and spirituality presented in Proverbs 16. How might the teachings in this chapter deepen one's connection with the divine?

Worship and Reverence (Proverbs 17):

Proverbs 17 touches on the relationship between worship and reverence. How can acts of worship be infused with a genuine spirit of reverence as discussed in this chapter?

Applying the Fear of the Lord (Proverbs 14 to 17):

Identify specific instances in Proverbs 14 to 17 where the fear of the Lord is linked to practical living. How can individuals apply these principles in their daily lives?

Practical Wisdom for Faithful Living (Proverbs 14 to 17):

Explore practical wisdom for faithful living found in Proverbs 14 to 17. How might these practical insights shape the way individuals approach their relationships, work, and personal growth?

Wisdom in Speech (Proverbs 14 to 17):

Discuss the role of speech and communication in faithful living, as highlighted in Proverbs 14 to 17. How can individuals ensure their words align with a life of reverence and wisdom?

Critical Thinking:

Analyze the cultural and historical context of Proverbs 14 to 17. How might the societal norms of the time influence the guidance provided on faithful living and the fear of the Lord?

Personal Application Challenges:

Identify specific challenges related to living a faithful life and cultivating the fear of the Lord. How might the principles in Proverbs 14 to 17 guide individuals in addressing these challenges?

Group Discussion:

Engage in a group discussion about the collective wisdom gained from Proverbs 14 to 17. How can the principles discussed contribute to a community that embraces faithful living and reverent worship?

Chapter 7: Navigating Challenges and Temptations (Proverbs 23 to 25)

Reflecting on Navigating Challenges:

How do Proverbs 23 to 25 contribute to our understanding of navigating challenges and resisting temptations? Share your insights and reflections on the principles presented in these chapters.

Introduction to Chapter 7:

Explore the opening verses of Proverbs 23. How do these verses set the tone for discussions on navigating challenges and resisting temptations in these chapters?

Overcoming Challenges with Wisdom (Proverbs 23):

Proverbs 23 addresses challenges related to wealth and excess. How can wisdom guide individuals in navigating challenges associated with materialism and societal pressures?

Resisting Temptation (Proverbs 24):

Discuss the wisdom presented in Proverbs 24 regarding resisting temptation. How might these principles be applied in the face of moral, ethical, or personal temptations?

Coping with Adversity (Proverbs 25):

Proverbs 25 provides insights into coping with adversity. How can individuals apply the wisdom in this chapter to navigate challenges and maintain resilience in the face of difficulties?

Balancing Individual Responsibility and Trust in God (Proverbs 23 to 25):

Reflect on the balance between individual responsibility and trust in God's guidance as presented in Proverbs 23 to 25. How can individuals maintain this delicate balance in various aspects of life?

Wisdom in Decision-Making (Proverbs 23 to 25):

Explore the role of wisdom in decision-making, especially in challenging circumstances. How can individuals ensure that their decisions align with the principles of Proverbs 23 to 25?

Practical Wisdom for Navigating Challenges (Proverbs 23 to 25):

Identify specific pieces of practical wisdom for navigating challenges found in Proverbs 23 to 25. How can these insights guide individuals in making sound decisions during difficult times?

Critical Thinking:

Analyze the cultural and historical context of Proverbs 23 to 25. How might the societal challenges of the time influence the guidance provided on navigating adversity and resisting temptation?

Personal Application Challenges:

Identify specific challenges or temptations in your life that resonate with the themes in Proverbs 23 to 25. How might the principles in these chapters guide you in overcoming these challenges?

Group Discussion:

Engage in a group discussion about the collective wisdom gained from Proverbs 23 to 25. How can the principles discussed contribute to a community that supports one another in navigating challenges and resisting temptations?

Chapter 8: A Life of Integrity and Character (Proverbs 26 to 28)

Reflecting on Integrity and Character:

How do Proverbs 26 to 28 contribute to our understanding of living a life of integrity and character? Share your insights and reflections on the principles presented in these chapters.

Introduction to Chapter 8:

Explore the opening verses of Proverbs 26. How do these verses set the tone for discussions on integrity and character in these chapters?

Developing Integrity and Character (Proverbs 26):

Proverbs 26 addresses the concept of a fool. How can individuals cultivate wisdom and integrity to avoid the pitfalls of foolish behavior, as outlined in this chapter?

Living a Moral and Ethical Life (Proverbs 27):

Discuss the teachings in Proverbs 27 regarding living a moral and ethical life. How do these principles influence one's interactions with others and personal decision-making?

The Role of Wisdom in Community (Proverbs 28):

Proverbs 28 explores the impact of the righteous and the wicked on a community. How can the wisdom presented in this chapter guide individuals in contributing positively to their communities?

Balancing Humility and Confidence (Proverbs 26 to 28):

Reflect on the balance between humility and confidence as discussed in Proverbs 26 to 28. How can individuals maintain humility while confidently living out their values?

Wisdom in Conflict Resolution (Proverbs 26 to 28):

Explore the wisdom provided in Proverbs 26 to 28 for resolving conflicts. How can individuals apply these principles to foster reconciliation and understanding in their relationships?

Practical Wisdom for Integrity (Proverbs 26 to 28):

Identify specific pieces of practical wisdom for maintaining integrity found in Proverbs 26 to 28. How can these insights guide individuals in making ethical decisions in various aspects of life?

Critical Thinking:

Analyze the cultural and historical context of Proverbs 26 to 28. How might the societal expectations of the time influence the guidance provided on living a life of integrity and character?

Personal Application Challenges:

Identify specific challenges related to maintaining integrity and character that you currently face. How might the principles in Proverbs 26 to 28 guide you in addressing these challenges?

Group Discussion:

Engage in a group discussion about the collective wisdom gained from Proverbs 26 to 28. How can the principles discussed contribute to a community that values and promotes integrity and character?

Chapter 9: Community and Servant Leadership (Proverbs 29 to 31)

Reflecting on Community and Leadership:

How do Proverbs 29 to 31 contribute to our understanding of community and servant leadership? Share your insights and reflections on the principles presented in these chapters.

Introduction to Chapter 9:

Explore the opening verses of Proverbs 29. How do these verses set the tone for discussions on community and servant leadership in these chapters?

Overview of Community and Servant Leadership (Proverbs 29 to 31):

Provide a general overview of the themes related to community and servant leadership found in Proverbs 29 to 31. How do these principles contribute to the development of a strong and harmonious community?

Understanding Leadership Responsibilities (Proverbs 29):

Proverbs 29 discusses the role of a ruler and the impact on the people. How can leaders, whether in government or other spheres, fulfill their responsibilities with wisdom and justice?

Leadership and Justice (Proverbs 30):

Explore the principles of justice and fairness presented in Proverbs 30. How can leaders ensure a just and equitable society, and how can individuals contribute to this vision?

Wise Governance (Proverbs 31):

Discuss the characteristics of the ideal wife in Proverbs 31. How might the qualities described be applied to leadership in various contexts, emphasizing wisdom, diligence, and compassion?

The Role of Wisdom in Community Building (Proverbs 29 to 31):

Reflect on the role of wisdom in community building and leadership. How can the principles of Proverbs 29 to 31 guide individuals in fostering positive relationships within a community?

Balancing Authority and Humility (Proverbs 29 to 31):

Explore the balance between authority and humility as discussed in Proverbs 29 to 31. How can leaders exercise authority while remaining humble and servant-hearted?

Practical Wisdom for Community Life (Proverbs 29 to 31):

Identify specific pieces of practical wisdom for building and sustaining a healthy community found in Proverbs 29 to 31. How can these insights be applied in various aspects of community life?

Critical Thinking:

Analyze the cultural and historical context of Proverbs 29 to 31. How might the societal norms of the time influence the guidance provided on community life and servant leadership?

Personal Application Challenges:

Identify specific challenges related to community building or leadership that you currently face. How might the principles in Proverbs 29 to 31 guide you in addressing these challenges?

Group Discussion:

Engage in a group discussion about the collective wisdom gained from Proverbs 29 to 31. How can the principles discussed contribute to building a community characterized by servant leadership and mutual support?

Suggestions for Future Study

Congratulations on completing the enlightening journey through the Book of Proverbs! As you continue your quest for wisdom and spiritual growth, here are some further reading recommendations and resources to deepen your understanding and application of the profound teachings we've explored:

"The Complete Guide to the Book of Proverbs: King Solomon Reveals the Secrets to Long Life, Riches, and Honor by Cody L. Jones

This comprehensive guide provides insights and commentary on each verse of Proverbs, offering additional perspectives to enhance your understanding.

"The Wisdom Literature: Interpreting Biblical Texts Series" by Richard J. Clifford:

Delve into the academic and theological aspects of Proverbs with this scholarly work. It provides a deeper analysis of the literary and cultural context of wisdom literature.

"Proverbs: Wisdom for Living" by Kevin Perrotta

Kevin Perrotta's book is an accessible and engaging exploration of Proverbs, providing practical applications for daily living and insights into the transformative power of wisdom.

"How to Read Proverbs" by Tremper Longman III:

This book offers guidance on understanding the literary structure and cultural nuances of Proverbs, equipping you with tools to delve even deeper into its wisdom.

Online Study Platforms:

Explore online platforms like BibleHub, Blue Letter Bible, or BibleGateway for commentaries, parallel translations, and additional resources to enhance your study of Proverbs.

Podcasts and Sermons:

Listen to podcasts or sermons on Proverbs from respected scholars and spiritual leaders. Many platforms offer insightful discussions that can provide new perspectives on familiar verses.

Join a Study Group or Online Community:

Engage with fellow seekers by joining a local study group or participating in online forums dedicated to the study of Proverbs. Sharing insights and learning from others can enrich your journey.

Explore Related Topics:

Consider exploring related topics such as biblical wisdom literature, ancient Near Eastern wisdom traditions, or topics addressed in Proverbs like justice, leadership, and ethics.

Practical Application Books:

Look for books that bridge the gap between ancient wisdom and modern living. Titles like "Living Well: God's Wisdom from the Book of Proverbs" by Allan Moseley provide practical applications.

Attend Seminars or Workshops:

Check local religious or educational institutions for seminars or workshops on the Book of Proverbs. These events often feature experts who provide in-depth insights and foster meaningful discussions.

Remember, your journey with Proverbs is not a solitary one. Seek the wisdom of others, explore different perspectives, and continue to apply the timeless truths you've discovered. May your ongoing exploration lead to a life deeply enriched by the wisdom that Proverbs offers.

Study Notes

Study Notes

Study Notes

Study Notes

Study Notes

About the Author

Debb Boom Wateren loves helping other people learn. She has done this in her time as an ESL educator, guiding many others through the joys and travails of learning English, and in her time as a project manager, navigating construction projects from concept to completion. A lifelong learner, she enjoys art, music, travel, history, reading, and libraries. She has a symbiotic learning relationship with her cat, Eleanor Roosevelt, named for one of her heroes. They both enjoy their home in the High Rocky Mountains, embracing life's new challenges together. Says Debb, "Attitude is the difference between an ordeal and an adventure." The originator of that quote is unknown, but Debb embraces it all the same.

DBW Best Books LLC

contact@DBWbestbooks.com

Thank you for reading and learning from this book. Please consider leaving an honest review.

Other Books by Debb Boom Wateren

Non-Fiction
Women Adventures and Explorers
Women Inventors, Scientists, and Discoverers
Women Breaking Barriers in Sport
Women Leaders in History
Proverbs for the 21st Century
Psalms for the 21st Century
Ecclesiastes for the 21st Century
Reimagining Matthew for the 21st Century
Marked for Today: A Contemporary Exploration of the Gospel o Mark for the 21st Century
Lucid Horizons: Navigating the Gospel of Luke in the 21st Century
The Game of Cricket for Spectators

Journals
Kindness: A Choice We Make Each Day
Travel Journal
Wine Tasting Journal
Prayer Journal
Writing Journals with Blank Pages
Daily Planner for Teens
Daily Planner for Adults: Flower Drawings to Inspire

Coloring Books and Activity Books for Adults
Fancy Decorated Eggs
Fantasy Animals and Birds
Elaborate Animals
Mandalas Book 1 and 2
Mazes
Picture Searches Book 1 and 2
Gnomes and Elves
Flower Gardens

Coloring Books for Children
Large Wild Birds
Construction
Firefighters
Music
Fun Animals
Space: Ages 4-8
Space: Ages 8-11
Gnomes and Elves and Where They Live

Made in the USA
Coppell, TX
23 November 2024

40853213R00050